The World of the Policy Analyst

CHATHAM HOUSE STUDIES IN POLITICAL THINKING
SERIES EDITOR: George J. Graham, Jr.
Vanderbilt University

The World of the Policy Analyst
Rationality, Values, and Politics

Robert A. Heineman
Alfred University

William T. Bluhm
University of Rochester

Steven A. Peterson
Alfred University

Edward N. Kearny
Western Kentucky University

CHATHAM HOUSE PUBLISHERS, INC.
Chatham, New Jersey

THE WORLD OF THE POLICY ANALYST

Chatham House Publishers, Inc.
Box One, Chatham, New Jersey 07928

Publisher: Edward Artinian
Cover design: Antler & Baldwin Design Group, Inc.
Composition: Bang, Motley, Olufsen
Printing and Binding: Banta Company

Library of Congress Cataloging-in-Publication Data

The World of the policy analyst: rationality, values, and politics /
Robert A. Heineman ... [et al.].
    p.   cm. — (Chatham House studies in political thinking)
Includes bibliographical references and index.
ISBN 0-934540-75-6
1. Policy sciences. I. Heineman, Robert A.   II. Series.
H97.W68   1990
320'.6—dc20   90-39484
                                                         CIP

Manufactured in the United States of America
10 9 8 7 6 5 4 3 2

Acknowledgments

This book has evolved, through the labor and advice of many people, over a period of several years. David Szczerbacki and Thomas Leitko provided sources and insights. Robert Thigpen, Duncan MacRae, Jr., and Roland Warren served as careful, critical readers and offered important suggestions. In their willingness to put in long hours at the word processor, Cheryl Monroe and Marlene Wightman could hardly be surpassed. Student assistants Thomas Conlon and David Ruller also helped in this respect, and the staff at Herrick Library did their usual efficient job of obtaining source materials. Finally, Alfred University provided important financial support for much of this project.

Each chapter was the responsibility of a single author, but the authors each read and edited the entire manuscript. The Introduction and chapters 1 and 6 were the responsibility of Robert Heineman. Steven A. Peterson had a similar relationship to chapters 2 and 4; William T. Bluhm dealt with chapter 3; and Edward N. Kearny focused on chapter 5.

This book is dedicated to the many students of the authors who work in the policy process and whose experiences have been an important stimulus for providing a comprehensive perspective on their roles in that process. As is customary and proper, the authors assume responsibility for those errors of rendition or judgment that may be contained herein.

Contents

Introduction

In recent years, policy analysis, as both an academic pursuit and a vocation, has grown in number of practitioners and in reputation. Major universities have instituted curricula centered on policy analysis, and a large amount of literature applying analytical techniques to social problems has been published. At all levels of government and at every stage of the policy process, analytical studies of problems and evaluations of programs have become commonplace. Yet despite the development of sophisticated methods of inquiry, policy analysis has not had a major substantive impact on policy makers. Policy analysts have remained distant from the power centers where policy decisions are made.

Concern about the limited influence of rational analysis in the policy process has had the effect of raising fundamental questions about the orientation and role of policy analysis. It now seems clear that to be politically influential, policy analysis must be practiced as an integral part of its broader cultural context. It is not, and cannot be, a separate "scientific" endeavor inherently entitled to the deference of politicians and citizens. Its practitioners must understand that they are both in and of a particular kind of political world and that to maximize their policy effectiveness they must acknowledge the characteristics of that world—that its decentralized, poorly coordinated political institutions enshrine and implement the values of a paradoxical political culture. This book is about these institutional and cultural contexts of policy analysis. The authors have tried to provide students of the policy-making process and future decision makers (policy analysts, administrators, legislators, judges) with a perspective for grasping the manifold dimensions of the world in which policy analysis takes place.

This work is not intended as a how-to-do-it book. Instead, it is a detailed analysis of the situation of the policy analyst. The intention of the authors is to help the analyst become more sensitive to the salient factors that influence the way he or she conceives and executes the task at hand. The goal of the book is therefore to illustrate the elements of scientific

1

rationality in the enterprise of policy analysis, the ways in which ultimate values and conceptions of moral right and wrong are intertwined with this approach, and the influence of decentralized institutions of political authority on attempts to implement rational moral purpose. The reader may find in this book suggestive clues about ways to become a more effective policy analyst. But the focus of this study is not on how to practice that vocation. It examines the difficult and complex context that practitioners must understand to be as effective as they can be.

This book has two primary purposes: (1) to contribute toward a more realistic understanding of policy analysis in the policy process by examining the normative assumptions that permeate policy analysis; and (2) to explain the essential elements of the political process with which analysts must be prepared to work if they expect their efforts to have reasonable chances for influence. At a minimum, this perspective should make policy analysis a more self-conscious process by encouraging analysts to be aware of the values behind the numbers and how these values necessarily shape the outcomes of both policy analysis and the policy process.

Recent analyses of democratic culture and political processes in America have questioned whether contemporary conditions permit the constructive resolution of social problems. With *The End of Liberalism*[1] in 1969, Theodore J. Lowi was one of the first to provide a thorough critique of the corrosive effects of "interest group liberalism" on the democratic policy process. Lowi, a political scientist, argued that the dominance of interest groups in the policy process had diluted the legitimacy of formal norms and procedures and had undermined the proper role of governmental authority. Government was rapidly becoming little more than an arena for the negotiation of interest-group demands. He concluded that in this context, neither rational planning nor meaningful standards of right and wrong were possible and that the nation was approaching a crisis in public authority. Others have concurred with Lowi's analysis.

Taking a broader perspective, Mancur Olson, an economist, has contended that in democracies, freedom of association inevitably leads to economic stagnation. Groups soon discover that manipulation of the government is easier and more profitable than competition in the open market. The scramble to use governmental powers and favors for narrow advantage engenders "an unending process of loophole discoveries and closures with the complexity and cost of regulation continually increasing."[2] Those who are successful in obtaining governmental protection become vested interests who resist change and stifle open competition in their areas. Adeptness at political manipulation—not efficient, competitive production and marketing —becomes the route to economic success.

A number of commentators have suggested that interest-group dominance in the policy process is leading to a pervasive value relativism. In *After Virtue,* Alasdair MacIntyre, a student of ethics, contends that society and government are enmeshed in the claims of emotivism, the belief that all moral judgments "are *nothing but* expressions of preference, expressions of attitude or feeling, insofar as they are moral or evaluative in character."[3] In his view, our pluralist culture "possesses no method of weighting, no rational criterion for deciding between claims based on legitimate entitlement against claims based on need."[4] MacIntyre is particularly harsh on claims that social science expertise can provide the knowledge and means for social change. In a statement perhaps more prescient than he intended, MacIntyre argues that the most effective bureaucrat "is the best actor."[5] In his view, dexterity in manipulating images and beliefs about science and government are the tools of effective power, not the specialized knowledge of policy expertise.

The implications of these assessments of the policy process have to be disturbing to the policy analyst no matter how intrepid he or she may be. In these views, interest-group power is elevating informal relationships and understandings to a level of influence and complexity that threatens to swamp the formal boundaries and procedures of constitutional government. Samuel P. Huntington's comment that in America "effective power is unnoticed power; power observed is power devalued"[6] speaks directly to this point. Under such conditions, the claims of those relying on rational analysis carry little weight when confronting interests adept at working within the interstices of the system. With no widely accepted sources of official or normative legitimacy, values (rational or irrational) become dependent on those with sufficient power to impose their definitions of morality. Group theorists did not cause the fragmentation of the American policy process, but, as thinkers like Lowi have recognized, their failure to provide a more comprehensive model of the political has contributed significantly to the diminution of expectations for American democracy once held by devotees of policy analysis as well as by the public at large.

Not surprisingly, many recent studies of American politics have been pessimistic in tone. Olson finds himself hoping and "searching for a happy ending."[7] Huntington concludes his survey of American political culture with the suggestion that America is not a failure but a "disappointment."[8] Studies dealing directly with the mechanics of the policy process follow a similar tack. At the beginning of his analysis of the implementation process, Eugene Bardach warns the unwary reader that "this is not an optimistic book."[9] In their earlier treatment of implementation, Jeffrey Pressman and Aaron Wildavsky noted that "the remarkable thing is that new programs work at all."[10] And in his text on the policy process, Thomas R. Dye asks, "Does government really know what it is doing?" and answers, "Generally speaking, no."[11] Obtaining a broader comprehension of the position of policy analysis in relation to these problems may facilitate understanding and, perhaps, mitigation of them.

The question of normative perspectives and assumptions deserves brief preliminary treatment. A number of commentators have noted the absence of discussion about fundamental values in policy analysis literature and curricula.[12] In a sense, such criticisms are inaccurate, for numerous works have examined ethical issues from a philosophical perspective. The problem has been that, while these discussions have helped to clarify and stimulate, they have tended to be of marginal practical use for the practicing policy analyst. Their exposition of ethical difficulties far too often concentrates on logical rigor, not on the conflicting, changing, and often irrational values that influence political decisions. Used carefully, however, they can demonstrate the limitations of purely utilitarian calculations. An example of this approach that has received some fame is the "trolley problem" stated by Judith Jarvis Thomson.[13]

In the trolley problem, Thomson hypothesizes a runaway trolley headed down a track with a spur. If the trolley remains on the main track, it will hit and probably kill five people. If the driver or a bystander diverts it to the spur, it will kill but one person. Elaborating on this hypothetical situation, Thomson postulates a variety of details and modifications from which she tries to extract moral lessons or generalizations. Models of this sort have important pedagogical uses in the appropriate context but are only tenuously linked to real life. Their fundamental danger is not so much their isolation from the real world as their tendency to suggest to students of analysis imbued with the virtues of analytical precision that values can be defined and approached with similar rigor. Unfortunately, the policy process already contains too many individuals who in their zealous pursuit of particular goals operate with cognitive blinders in their approaches to issues and problems. Far more important to the policy analyst is an understanding of the fundamental, culturally determined normative expectations that inform those who will respond to or be affected by his or her suggestions. In this respect, the policy analyst needs to recognize that contradictory beliefs and irrational positions are not aberrations but inherent facts of the political system that have to be confronted with both flexibility and persuasion.

In the discussions that follow, the term *values* will be used to describe beliefs and attitudes that guide individual behavior in the policy process. These beliefs and attitudes can be divided into three general categories ranging from broad cultural forces to orientations that are specific to individuals. The least definable and articulate of these categories includes cultural norms and expectations that have deep roots in American culture and that are usually uncritically accepted as valid. Closely related to these and originating from them are ideological positions that provide rationalizations for particular policy views. A reasonably distinct and different set of values can be identified as those positions formed by one's role in the policy process. Agencies, legislative bodies, courts, and interest groups have all developed norms and expectations about goals and appropriate forms of behavior. Policy actors will naturally tend to respond to issues within the framework of the norms and expectations of the institution or organization with which they are affiliated. Although these may appear peripheral to substantive policy issues, they are often in fact determinative of policy decisions. Finally, at the most specific level are those personal beliefs and attitudes that vary from individual to individual. These would include desire for power or fame, concern for integrity, and pursuit of wealth or security. As they are used in this work, values will refer to one of the three categories just described, and in each instance the context should make clear which of these concepts is being considered.

This book assumes a broad definition of policy analysis. It recognizes that analysis relevant to understanding the policy process and to policy decisions may be undertaken from a number of useful viewpoints. Physicians, attorneys, or chemists, if they are working to provide input to policy decisions, could in this capacity be seen as doing policy analysis.[14] The very concept of analysis, of course, presupposes the importance of rational argument and rigorous methodology, and in this respect policy analysis must be differentiated from approaches to the policy process that do not meet, or make minimal use of, these criteria.

Within these broad parameters, considerable diversity exists. Duncan MacRae, Jr., argues that policy analysis should be seen as an "applied discipline." From his perspective, policy analysis is concerned with "the constructive analysis of concrete policy choices through research and effective policy advice."[15] Asserting that his use of the term "policy studies" is the same as MacRae's idea of policy analysis, William D. Coplin sees policy

studies as "the application of the social sciences to societal problems."[16]
Another, broader view of policy analysis has been offered by Thomas R.
Dye, who views policy analysis as more concerned with understanding and
explaining policy issues. Policy analysts should strive for generally applicable explanations, or theories, of policy issues because "developing scientific knowledge about the forces shaping public policy and the consequences
of public policy is itself a socially relevant activity."[17] The authors conceive
of policy analysis in the larger sense of encompassing the application of
analytical techniques to social issues for the purpose of both enhanced understanding and improved input into the policy process. In this respect,
their concept is close to the broad view first suggested by Yehezkel Dror.[18]

At this stage in the development of approaches to policy analysis,
restrictive delineation of what legitimately constitutes policy analysis can
easily be more harmful than helpful. The recent attempts by some scholars
to distinguish between policy analysis and evaluation research do not at this
time seem to be sustainable.[19] Policy analysis requires evaluation as an integral part of the continuing cycle of input into policy decisions. But more
important, those trained outside the usual disciplines that contribute to
schools of policy analysis should be encouraged also to see themselves as
analytic contributors to public policy and should have available to them the
means for gaining a better understanding and perspective on their position.
Policy analysis as a field of endeavor, whether applied or theoretical, is
developing techniques and models that may give it a more specific identity
and expertise. But the perspective being urged here should be useful and
comprehensible to anyone who expects to provide analytical input into the
decision-making process.

The reader will discover that this book moves from the general, broad
issues raised by the emergence of policy analysis to the particulars of the
policy process itself. First, the American cultural roots of the ideal of rational social analysis are examined. This is followed by a discussion of some
of the important techniques of policy analysis in terms of the assumptions
that are essential, although often unarticulated, to them and in terms of
their relationship to decision making. Then leading American values are
analyzed with reference to their historical development, their present paradoxical character, and the way they fit into recent efforts to analyze sys-
tematically the ethical dilemmas in policy analysis. The importance of
norms and their effects on political behavior are next illustrated through examination of recent trends in the electorate. This discussion moves naturally
into the problems posed to policy recommendations by fragmented policy-

making institutions. The courts are treated separately because they differ in important respects from the elected branches in their response to policy analysis and policy issues. In conclusion, proposals for structural reform of the policy process are examined. These are followed by tentative suggestions as to how policy analysis might be made more effective in the policy process and analysts might integrate normative considerations into the specifics of their work.

Obviously, the student is free to pick and choose as he or she sees fit from the ideas offered, but the intent is to provide a broad cultural understanding of the American policy process that will produce a more comprehensive and realistic conception of policy studies than the specialized studies that dominate the field. The aim is not to denigrate the need for rigorous analysis of social problems but to enhance understanding of the capabilities and limits of policy analysis by placing it in the context in which it functions.

Notes

1. Theodore J. Lowi, *The End of Liberalism*, 2d ed. (New York: Norton, 1979).

2. Mancur Olson, *The Rise and Decline of Nations* (New Haven: Yale University Press, 1982), 70.

3. Alasdair MacIntyre, *After Virtue* (Notre Dame, Ind.: University of Notre Dame Press, 1981), 11.

4. Ibid., 229.

5. Ibid., 102.

6. Samuel P. Huntington, *American Politics* (Cambridge, Mass.: Harvard University Press, 1981), 75.

7. Olson, *Rise and Decline of Nations*, 237.

8. Huntington, *American Politics*, 262.

9. Eugene Bardach, *The Implementation Game* (Cambridge, Mass: MIT Press, 1978), 6.

10. Jeffrey T. Pressman and Aaron Wildavsky, *Implementation*, 2d ed. (Berkeley: University of California Press, 1979), 109.

11. Thomas R. Dye, *Understanding Public Policy*, 6th ed. (Englewood Cliffs, N.J.: Prentice-Hall, 1987), 350.

12. Rosemarie Tong, *Ethics in Public Policy* (Englewood Cliffs, N.J.: Prentice-Hall, 1986), xi; Ira Katznelson, "Rethinking the Silences of Social and

Economic Policy," *Political Science Quarterly* 101 (1986): 310–13; Bruce L. Payne, "Contexts and Epiphanies: Policy Analysis and the Humanities," *Journal of Policy Analysis and Management* 4 (Fall 1984): 96; Douglas J. Amy, "Why Policy Analysis and Ethics Are Incompatible," *Journal of Policy Analysis and Management* 3 (Summer 1984): 573–91.

13. Judith Jarvis Thomson, *Rights, Restitution, and Risk,* ed. William Parent (Cambridge, Mass.: Harvard University Press, 1986), 94–116.

14. Tong, *Ethics,* 41, notes, "To the degree that the roles of the policy analyst and the subject-area specialist are increasingly indiscernible, so too is it more and more difficult to articulate how a policy advisor differs from a policy analyst or a policy specialist."

15. Duncan MacRae, Jr., *The Social Function of Social Science* (New Haven: Yale University Press, 1976), 305–6; Duncan MacRae, Jr., "Introducing Undergraduates to Public Policy Analysis by the Case Method," in *Teaching Policy Studies,* ed. William D. Coplin (Lexington, Mass.: D.C. Heath, 1978), 129–30.

16. William D. Coplin, ed., *Teaching Policy Studies* (Lexington, Mass.: D.C. Heath, 1978), xv.

17. Dye, *Understanding Public Policy,* 7–8.

18. Yehezkel Dror, "Policy Analysts: A New Professional Role in Government Service," *Public Administration Review* 27 (September 1967): 200–203.

19. Frank Fischer, "Policy Expertise and the 'New Class,'" in *Confronting Values in Policy Analysis,* ed. Frank Fischer and John Forester (Newbury Park, Calif.: Sage, 1987), 94–126.

CHAPTER 1

The Emergence of a Field

A commitment to science and its methods as the most important source of progress has permeated scholarly assumptions about the possibility of a social science. This view and the cultural heritage of American social science have both been exceptionally important influences on the development of policy analysis. Yet today policy analysts find themselves confronting a policy process that is unable to utilize effectively the sophisticated methodologies and related technology that have been developed to examine social issues. Except during rare periods of national crisis, policy analysts have seen recommendations that they have justified on the basis of rational merit submerged in a policy process marked by the proliferation of organized interests and by the growth of institutional complexity and fragmentation. In this context, the values of analytical rigor and logic have given way to political necessities.

The Historical Background

In most important respects, the origins of the anomalous position of policy analysis can be traced to intellectual and social developments that first became salient and began to affect political thinking during the latter part of the nineteenth century. The emergence of increased concern for greater analytical rigor in the study of individual and social behavior provides one of the important sources of contemporary ideas about social science which in turn have engendered policy analysis as an identifiable endeavor. Basic to these changes was the belief that rational, scientific methods could be applied to the improvement of social conditions. The growth of large industrial organizations led to efforts to control human behavior in the interests of increased efficiency and profit, and Frederick W. Taylor remains famous for his formulation of the principles of scientific management around the turn of the century. Additionally, new views of science, influ-

9

enced heavily by Charles Darwin, which emphasized change and evolving concepts of truth, were used by philosophers and social scientists to buttress their efforts at social reform. Scientific approaches began to be applied directly to social activity and were seen as particularly useful to efforts to improve society.

The Era of Reform

These ideas moved rather quickly into the realm of public policy and led to what Russell Hanson has termed the "rationalization" of political discourse.[1] The criterion of efficiency was seen as equally applicable to industry and government, and it became fashionable to argue that administration in government should be separated from "politics." Many of these ideas culminated in the Progressive movement, which, although it did not establish extensive welfare programs, did contribute significantly to an increase in government regulatory efforts. Legislation establishing such agencies as the Federal Reserve Board and the Federal Trade Commission along with other major regulatory legislation gave clear indications that the American public was willing to accept government intervention in the private sphere on a much larger scale than ever before. Of particular note was the public's willingness to make the regulatory agencies "independent" by insulating them from the political pressures faced by other agencies. This approach signaled a new deference to experts in the areas being regulated.

This period also marks the beginning of the professionalization of academic social science. This movement was linked closely to the actively reformist motivations of scholars dissatisfied with social conditions and confident in their ability to fashion improvements. Another contributing element was the influence of German ideas on American social scientists. Many Americans studied in Germany, where they saw firsthand the effects of Bismarck's welfare measures and were exposed to the power of the historical method in social analysis. Reflecting on his German educational experience, William Graham Sumner, himself a critic of reform, asserted that the German "method of study was nobly scientific, and was worthy to rank, both for its results and its discipline, with the best of the natural science methods."[2] As a result of these experiences, reform-minded students of society tended to be sympathetic to criticism of the limitations that the laissez-faire doctrines of Herbert Spencer and the classical economists imposed on government. Between 1886 and 1895, no less than six major social science journals were established to assist in the propagation of social science expertise, and by the early 1900s major graduate schools in the

United States had assumed the responsibility of preparing social scientists to assist in the formulation of governmental policy.[3]

Dewey's Influence
Probably the single most influential source of intellectual support for the application of rational analysis to social problems in the cause of reform was the thought of John Dewey. Richard Bernstein believes that Dewey's ideas constituted a "distinctive intellectual expression of American culture"[4] and asserts that from the 1890s Dewey was America's intellectual spokesman for practical social reform. Dewey argued that no useful metaphysical absolutes exist. Philosophy and science contribute to truth and progress only as they are applied to changing human conditions. Social scientists must not hesitate to apply the experimental method to social problems. The criteria of truth are grounded in the feelings of individuals in society, and the validity of ideas and social institutions is properly judged by the degree to which they contribute to the improvement of life.

In works like *The Public and Its Problems*[5] Dewey expressed a tremendous amount of faith in the ability of organized social interests to articulate public values and effect social reform. For him, government was simply a larger form of organized public interest and as such was subject to the limits and demands made on it by the citizenry. Dewey's support of democratic processes, his application of the scientific perspective to social issues, and his focus on immediate, practical problems appealed to Americans generally and provided philosophical legitimacy for the efforts of social scientists.

In retrospect, one of the most important works for understanding the intellectual lineage of the modern policy analyst in more rigorous social science and for grasping the political effects of the ideas fostered by Dewey was Arthur F. Bentley's *The Process of Government*. Bentley disdained formalism and metaphysical concepts in favor of description of the dynamics of the political process. "We must deal with felt things, not with feelings, with intelligent life, not with idea ghosts."[6] The source of facts, the bedrock of usable data, was group activity. Human behavior was describable and definable only in terms of activity: "There is no idea which is not a reflection of social activity,"[7] and that activity is group activity. Thus, for Bentley, "When the groups are stated, everything is adequately stated,"[8] and he proceeded to describe the political scene of his time in terms of group activity.

Bentley's group approach did not come into vogue among political scientists until after World War II, with the rise to prominence of pluralist interpretations of the political process. But in terms of the early twentieth century, his treatment of politics is important for the insight that it provides into the wide influence of Dewey's ideas and for its reflection of contemporary thinking about the contours of scientific social analysis. Dewey's impact is especially apparent in Bentley's rejection of any form of metaphysical absolutes, or "idea ghosts," and in his choice of group activity as the essential datum of human life. More important, perhaps, for an understanding of the development of policy analysis was Bentley's stance of normative neutrality. Unlike Dewey, Bentley was simply interested in the facts. He made no judgments as to the worth or lack thereof of group activities. He tried to remove himself from any hint of social activism or reform. For him, science demanded no less.

Of more immediate impact on public policy was Dewey's influence on judicial thinking. In particular, Dewey's advocacy of experimental social planning translated readily into Roscoe Pound's concept of social engineering. Pound, dean of Harvard Law School and a major legal thinker, argued that judges should be aware that "continual changes in the circumstances of social life demand continual adjustments to the pressure of social interests."[9] Following Dewey's approach, Pound insisted that judges should move from behind the facade of formal, abstract legal logic and make judicial policy that deals accurately with the social facts involved in a particular case. Additionally, he urged that judges enlist social scientists in their efforts to work social reform through judicial decisions.

Value Neutrality

Although it arose in a context of social reform, by the early twentieth century social science had withdrawn from advocacy of reform into a more comfortable posture of scientific objectivity, or value neutrality. The reasons for this were various and the consequences profound for both democratic society and its students. Many social scientists sincerely felt that their proper role in analysis was that of objective technician. In important respects, their position was bolstered by Dewey, who, although he was concerned about social reform, consistently refused in his extensive writings to articulate any substantive normative positions. Although not value neutral in the broadest sense, the Progressive movement, while supporting specific reforms, tended toward nonpartisanship in its emphasis on efficiency in government. Robert Scott and Arnold Shore note, for example, that Herbert Hoover, who as President was more supportive of the concept of scientific social analysis than any chief executive before or since, maintained a strict nonpartisan stance right up to the eve of the 1928 party nominating conventions.[10]

Mary Furner has argued persuasively that, in addition to these general cultural currents, academic social scientists advocating social reform were hard hit by challenges to their jobs and academic freedom made by corporate interests and their allies in higher education during the late nineteenth century.[11] The tribulations suffered by some of these leading activist social scientists made plain to their academic brethren that social advocacy carried with it the potential for direct personal hardship. Although exceptions to the general rule continued to occur throughout the twentieth century, by World War I social activism and objective social analysis were generally seen as incompatible. Scholars served in many official and advisory capacities in government at this time, but the accepted view argued that the scientific element in social science required the linkage of rigorous analysis with the avoidance of overt partisanship.

Unfortunately for the analysis of policy and the health of democratic processes, the move toward scientific objectivity spawned a denigration of the importance of values. Whether social scientists articulated them or not, values remained embedded in their methodological techniques as well as in the policy process. Their unwillingness to confront the normative aspects of their fields of study created a misleading conception of political reality and led to such artificial distinctions as the separation of administration from politics. As a result, social scientists rendered their work less relevant for those moving the levers of the policy process and by default contributed to the emergence of a political system that became increasingly subservient to the narrow demands of organized interests. Social scientists were in effect left tiptoeing along the edges of the moral claims of reform and the practicalities of politics, refusing to recognize the importance of either.

The New Deal
After the Progressive era, the New Deal was the next instance of major governmental reform, and it confirmed the propensity of reform efforts to fit comfortably within the instrumentalist ideas articulated by Dewey. Raymond Moley, Rexford Tugwell, and Adolf A. Berle, Jr., members of Franklin Roosevelt's Brain Trust, came to the administration from Columbia University, where Dewey was now teaching, having moved there from the University of Chicago in 1904. These advisers to FDR embraced the importance of organizational activity for dealing with economic problems. This approach to reform closely followed Dewey's suggestion that interest

organization in society should be encouraged. By integrating this idea in major legislation, New Deal leaders moved it beyond the private sector and in effect gave official recognition to the group interpretation of American politics.[12] The National Industrial Recovery Act, the Agricultural Adjustment Act, and the National Labor Relations Act all encouraged organization among economic interests in an effort to improve their positions by making them more effective in the policy process as well as their particular spheres of private activity. In these and other programs, social scientists played important roles as technicians and advisers, but as foot soldiers in the effort at recovery they remained removed from advocacy positions or attachment to encompassing normative goals.

The New Deal program has often been characterized as a pragmatic reaction to specific economic problems rather than the implementation of a coherent theory. In this respect, it demonstrated both the strengths and weaknesses of the narrowed focus encouraged by many social scientists. On the plus side, the New Deal reconfirmed the ability of Americans to act decisively and effectively in dealing with immediate problems. On the negative side, any commitment to long-range planning and goals that existed foundered on the power of special interests that encouraged the proliferation of programs that overlapped and occasionally conflicted with one another.[13]

From Technique to Policy Analysis

In the postwar era, a number of developments combined to give policy analysis greater status. At perhaps the most general and fundamental level, the movement of scientific issues onto the national policy agenda to an increasing degree created a climate in which analytical approaches to policy problems became more important. These approaches were integrated into the formal policy process by new policy initiatives, especially those fostered by the Johnson administration. Within higher education, the social science disciplines began to focus on dealing with social problems and on describing the policy process itself more objectively. But their perceived inability to be effective in the changing policy environment stimulated the emergence of policy studies as a distinct field of study that drew on contributions from a variety of disciplines. Within the general framework of this policy studies approach, the importance of rigorous analysis to improved understanding of the policy process and better decision making became recognized.

The Impact of Science

Efforts at social reform and attempts of social scientists to formulate value-free models of the public policy process have not been the only sources of support for policy analysis in recent years. Since World War II, advances in the natural sciences have caused significant modifications in governmental structure and in policy goals and processes. Jurgen Schmandt and James Everett Katz contend that during this period Americans have experienced a transition from an administrative welfare state to a scientific state.[14] Today, national policy makers must cope with an agenda that is heavily loaded with difficult scientific issues. These include exceedingly complex questions about nuclear and nonnuclear weapons systems, environmental protection, automation and the economy, space research, and energy resources.

The salience of scientific issues on the national agenda has influenced how policy makers frame their goals as well as their methods for approaching them. Schmandt and Katz predict that in the age of the scientific state, "we can expect scientific and technological thoughtways to slowly permeate the language, culture, and conceptual processes of at least middle-level policy makers, if not the highest echelons of governmental leadership."[15] The language and conceptual apparatus of science encourage policy makers to think in terms of goals that can be quantified and to give greater consideration to rigorous analytical arguments: "The tools of science—the evidence and the methods of research—become parts of the policy battles. The use of advisers and panels, reports and studies, research findings and data analyses are and increasingly will be important weapons in policy battles."[16] Finally, the concern with scientific questions has led to changes in institutional structures. The national government now has a number of agencies that have been created for the specific purpose of making science policy, and throughout the bureaucracy, other agencies have added units for research and development and program evaluation.

Policy analysis has historical roots in the development of the social sciences, but the emergence of the physical sciences as an important part of the public agenda has created a policy environment where rigorous analysis of problems is required and demanded. This does not mean that the additional impetus behind policy analysis will enhance its articulation with policy decisions. Schmandt and Katz caution: "Of particular concern here is the extent to which the technical functions of assessment and analysis become substitutes for decisionmaking, feeding a demand for ever more research and analysis while the decision point continues to recede."[17] Despite the growing hegemony of a scientific perspective in the policy arena, coordination of democratic processes with the contributions, methods, and challenges of the sciences remains an essential task for social scientists and policy makers.

Analysis and Policy

World War II stimulated the development of techniques that remain important to policy analysis. Chief among these was operations research, which was later tied into the broader analytical perspective of systems analysis. Operations research tended to be heavily quantitative and focused on narrow, specific problems such as the optimum deployment of defense weaponry, men, or materials. Working within a framework of normative consensus, analysts could concentrate on the technical aspects of problems and were able to produce noteworthy results. The improvement of computer technology and the development of additional tools (e.g., linear programming) have made operations research an even more powerful analytical approach. In times of peace, however, normative consensus weakens, and analysts must contend with the controversy and conflict that characterize democratic politics.

The relevance of social analysis for public policy was brought to public attention in dramatic fashion in the Supreme Court's decision in *Brown* v. *Board of Education* (1954). In arriving at their decision to rule racial segregation in public education unconstitutional, the Court had commissioned social science studies of the effects of racial segregation on children and society at large. In his opinion, Chief Justice Earl Warren drew on these and previous studies, and in doing so seemed to be accepting the idea, advanced earlier by Pound and Dewey, among others, that courts should use the social sciences to implement reforms. Whether social science analysis persuaded the Court to overturn segregation or whether it merely served the more symbolic role of bolstering an already determined decision, remains a nice question. But, whatever the case on this issue, the Court's apparent reliance on social science brought its practitioners public notoriety. Social scientists were criticized by segregationists led by a rampaging Governor George Wallace, who was to make "pointy-headed professors" the focus of many of his attacks. In contrast, those hoping to use analytical expertise in the cause of continued social reform were encouraged by the Court's recognition of their efforts.

The 1960s appear to be the next period that was crucial to the development of policy analysis. Particularly important at this time was the movement of Robert McNamara and his "whiz kids" into leadership positions in the Defense Department. Impressed by the contribution of analytical techniques to better decision making, these officials introduced a wide range of methods into the analysis of management and policy issues in the military.[18] They included cost-benefit analysis; operations and systems research; linear programming; and the planning, programming, budgeting system (PPBS). The latter so impressed President Lyndon Johnson with its potential for better management control that in August 1965 he ordered it implemented throughout the federal government. This directive was stymied by unenthusiastic budget officers and the difficulty in applying the concept on a large scale to domestic programs, and was finally voided by President Richard Nixon.[19] Despite opposition both within and outside the Defense Department to the application of analytical methods to problems, the McNamara people established clearly that there was a body of knowledge constituting policy analysis and gave it the legitimacy of official recognition.

While the McNamara approach was in many ways a key breakthrough toward public recognition and acceptance of policy analysis, relevant disciplines in the social sciences had since World War II also been undergoing debates and changes that moved them closer to becoming contributors to policy analysis. In sociology, an applied orientation to the study of society was being implemented by scholars like Paul Lazarsfeld, who demonstrated that analytical techniques, especially those utilizing survey research, had uses in private industry and public policy.[20] Lazarsfeld's activities provoked debate between sociologists favoring a more theoretical stance for their discipline and those wishing to see sociological ideas and analyses applied in society, an argument that in many ways reiterated issues that had been contested at the turn of the century. Political scientists until well into the 1960s found themselves struggling with a "behavioral revolution" that focused attention on the application of quantitative techniques to empirical political data, a movement to which Lazarsfeld's work in voting studies also contributed. But political scientists also began to feel the tug of "relevance." In his 1969 presidential address to the American Political Science Association, David Easton called for a "post-behavioral" approach that crossed disciplinary boundaries and moved toward dealing with social problems.[21]

The discipline of economics, however, rapidly outdistanced other social science disciplines in status as an important source of ideas and methodologies for public policy. John Maynard Keynes's ideas had provided economic theory with coherence and what has been termed a "robustness" that enabled it to retain applicability in the uncertain conditions of the real world. Additionally, within the framework of their general theories, economists were successful in innovating quantitative techniques, such as cost-benefit analysis, that delimited alternative approaches to problems. The discipline in fact gained official stature with the establishment of the Council of Economic Advisers in the Employment Act of 1946.

By the time of the Johnson administration, germination of the concept of a broader policy perspective had begun among scholars in the social sciences. Political scientists, for example, found the narrow focus of behavioralism not very useful in anticipating issues like the civil rights movement or the Vietnam war and began to look toward more inclusive paradigms. Harold Lasswell was especially active in moving the social sciences toward a policy focus, and in a 1951 article on the subject, he appears to have coined the term "policy sciences."[22]

It was Yehezkel Dror, however, who at an early stage in the increased concern with policy suggested a role for policy analysis specifically. Dror in the late 1960s was concerned about the degree to which the techniques and assumptions of economists had become part of the analyses on which public officials depended.[23] He pointed out that there was need for a perspective broader than that provided by the prevailing systems analysis approach. Moving beyond the application of technical analysis to specific problems, a policy analysis orientation would include consideration of intangible cultural factors, political problems, and organizational variables that should make studies more useful to policy makers. Finally, from 1967 through 1970, with the assistance of major private foundations, graduate programs in public policy were initiated at Harvard, Berkeley, Carnegie-Mellon, the Rand Graduate Institute, and the Universities of Michigan, Pennsylvania, Minnesota, and Texas.[24] In the next decade, at least thirteen journals in policy studies and policy analysis were begun. This period saw also the founding of the Policy Studies Organization and the Association for Public Policy Analysis and Management.

Policy analysis came of age during the days of the Great Society, and, as with many maturing processes, this change carried with it both wisdom and frustration gained from experience. The administration's efforts at large-scale social intervention engendered an enormous increase in employment opportunities for social scientists, and its funding of higher education provided a stimulus for the establishment of graduate programs in policy analysis and policy studies.[25] At the same time, the Great Society acted on the basis of interpretations of society and politics that suffered from unwarranted faith in scientific rationality. The advocates of analytical prowess were soon brought face to face with the realities of political power. As one commentator has noted, "in the Johnson years the policies of all those brilliant apostles of rationality gradually lost sight of the most elementary common sense"[26] with the result that their noses were bloodied badly in some instances. Of more fundamental importance and long-term significance was the lack of attention given to normative goals and assumptions about American society. In essence, policy analysis found itself in harness with goals often no more tangible than those of "good intentions." Here the consequences of inattention to cultural and political expectations were sufficiently disastrous to place the proponents of government-sponsored social reform on the defensive for at least the next two decades.

Analysis and Ideology

Belief in the efficacy of social science knowledge was deeply embedded in the assumptions of the architects of the Great Society programs. Even before the Kennedy administration, the Ford Foundation had funded efforts to apply social science knowledge to designated "gray areas" in cities in an attempt to prevent these marginally blighted urban enclaves from deteriorating into slums.[27] The Kennedy administration accepted the need for greater governmental intervention and made some movement in that direction, but it was President Johnson who was given the historic opportunity to flex the resources of the national government to their maximum on behalf of social reform.

The Great Society planners were particularly impressed by the ability of organized interests to work successfully in the policy process. Some of this attitude may have harkened back to New Deal programs, especially those fostering labor organization. Additionally, group interpretations of politics indicated that agencies and legislators responded most sympathetically to organized interests. Equally important to President Johnson's assistants had to be their experience with the influence that organization had brought to the black movement. Thus it was natural for the Johnson administration to assume that the route to greater political effectiveness and more social justice for the disadvantaged lay through organization that would enable them to compete with other groups in the policy process. The result was a conscious attempt through the War on Poverty to use government programs to organize the poor in what has been described as "a distinctive managerial kind of politics" directed by the White House.[28] These efforts were exemplified by requirements for citizen participation at the local level in the allocation of funds for most programs, whatever the socioeconomic status of their recipients.

Faith in the effectiveness of social science as a support for reform reflected assumptions that had been part of what might be termed the "culture" of social science throughout the twentieth century. What the Johnson people were soon to learn to their discomfort was that analysis of social conditions and policy need not necessarily result in findings sustaining the merits of their approach to social change. First they had the unpleasant experience of having their own policy people criticize their programs. In the words of Carol Hirschon Weiss, "The news was dismaying. Nothing seemed to be working as expected. The programs launched with such great hopes and fanfare did not appear to be attaining their objectives to alter poor people's lives."[29] Then they were subjected to the equally difficult experience of having the tools of social analysis turned on them by their ideological opponents. Edward Banfield's *The Unheavenly City* [30] was a broad attack on programs of federal social intervention, and the establishment of *The Public Interest* provided neoconservatives with a continuing forum for their views.

The Johnson administration could perhaps have weathered the critiques of their own analysts better if their programs had developed stronger political affiliations. But President Johnson had tried to move beyond incremental change by formulating many of his programs outside the usual policy process.[31] By relying heavily on task groups external to the bureaucracy, Johnson was able to obtain new ideas, but at the cost of political support. Subsequently, the old-line agencies chosen to implement these new programs had little attachment to their success, and similar sentiments existed in Congress. Meanwhile, the burgeoning interest in policy studies had given rise to an increased application of program evaluation that, when applied to the Great Society initiatives, uncovered numerous shortcomings and a lack of tangible results.[32] In a context of strong political programmatic support, these findings could have been used to improve programs. But in this instance, the initial failure to maximize political support rendered the Great Society efforts particularly vulnerable to political attack. Instead of assisting in the improvement of social reform, the conclusions of policy analysts tended to give greater credence to the suspicions of already uneasy politicians.

Attacks by the conservatives and neoconservatives were even more devastating than those of occasional supporters of the Great Society because they combined the use of analytical techniques with criticism of the unexamined assumptions about society that had accompanied reform efforts throughout the twentieth century. The conservative reaction to active government had been growing since World War II, and think tanks such as the

Heritage Foundation and the American Enterprise Institute provided scholars with additional bases from which to formulate their criticisms of reformist government. Conservatively inclined thinkers such as Edward Banfield, Daniel Patrick Moynihan, and James Q. Wilson demonstrated conclusively that policy analysis was not solely the province of social engineers. Banfield's widely read *Unheavenly City*, for example, drew on social science findings relating to poverty, race, health, education, housing, employment, and crime in attacking most of the Great Society's programs. But the really telling element in the positions of these scholars and their colleagues was not their use of analysis but their insistence on examining the assumptions about human nature and behavior that seemed to be the basis for reform efforts. These thinkers directly challenged the egalitarian optimism that had suffused reform, and in doing so, they served notice that in the United States, policy analysis could no longer be considered the exclusive resource of any particular ideology.

The focus on philosophical and sociological assumptions raised reservations about the accuracy of the group-oriented or, in social scientist terms, pluralist model of politics that had become prominent in both scholarly discussion and official policy. Much of the intellectual basis for this model could be traced to David B. Truman's *The Governmental Process*,[33] which with its publication in 1951 revived the interpretation of American politics first suggested by Bentley. Although Truman suggested that interest-group competition could incapacitate governmental policy, he gave far more attention to the merits of group activity. He argued that democratic processes would be protected from extremes of group conflict by the existence of latent, unorganized groups that would spring into being if one interest became too powerful or threatened the "rules of the game." Protection was also to be found in overlapping group memberships by individuals that had the effect of limiting the demands and activities of group leaders. Questions about this perspective came from both the ideological left and right. In both instances, they raised normative issues that Truman's posture of value neutrality avoided. The left tended to be concerned that a pluralist model of politics gave de facto legitimacy to organized interests over those unable to organize. The right was more concerned that a pluralist conception of politics moved moral judgment to the status of political compromise. These debates were accompanied by the somber spectacle of a government rendered increasingly impotent by the ability of organized interests to overcome the constitutional authority of institutional processes.

The interest-group interpretation illustrated another facet of the unwillingness of the social sciences to look beyond tangible, measurable activity. That this stance had ramifications for understanding of the public policy process generally was demonstrated by Charles Lindblom's article "The Science of 'Muddling Through.'"[34] Written in 1959, Lindblom's article has become a classic for its statement and defense of incremental decision making. What has been less noted has been the extent to which Lindblom drew on the group perspective in this seminal piece. As with the group theorists, Lindblom grounded values in the behavior of particular political actors. It made good sense, he argued, for administrators to eschew long-range goals in favor of immediate problems. In dealing with short-term goals, the official can more easily identify and operationalize the values conducive to the result to be achieved. The pluralistic system, he asserted, will ensure that interests are not ignored in this process: "Almost every interest has its watchdog.... It can be argued that our system often can assure a more comprehensive regard for the values of the whole society than any attempt at intellectual comprehensiveness."[35] In fact, it is wrongheaded to conceive of only long-term planning as rational: "Even partisanship and narrowness, to use pejorative terms, will sometimes be assets to rational decision-making, for they can doubly insure that what one agency neglects, another will not."[36] In "The Science of 'Muddling Through,'" Lindblom raised to a level of rational legitimacy the fragmented, halting, incremental approach to decision making characteristic of the American policy process and in doing so relied heavily on arguments previously made by the group theorists.

Science and Truth
The years of the Great Society programs provided the context in which policy studies and policy analysis became endeavors in which the national government invested both great hope and copious resources. Political scientists and sociologists moved to follow the lead of the economists in the hope that they, too, could become more relevant to decision making by applying their methodologies to the analysis of important social issues. As the grand plans of the initiators of the Great Society foundered on the shoals of political reaction and bureaucratic fragmentation, reliance on rational, analytic methods could not provide policy analysts with sufficient status or power to cope with political interests.

Social scientists and, more recently, policy analysts have often assumed that the objective, scientific quality of their analyses would carry weight in the policy process and protect them from the effects of political partisanship. Because it rests on a superficial view of the scientific enterprise and a faulty conception of the policy process, such a posture can lead to considerable frustration for the practitioner of policy analysis. While policy analysis can contribute significantly to the improvement of political decisions, critics from a broad range of disciplines have shown that analytical methodologies cannot provide scientific, objective answers to policy issues. Unfortunately, in important respects, policy analysis has suffered unfairly from expectations about its policy role and scientific capabilities, and it is therefore essential that today's policy analyst have an understanding of prevailing interpretations of scientific endeavor and the political components of the policy process.

Although the knowledge may not be essential to their day-to-day work, students of policy analysis should have at least an awareness of current critiques of the physical sciences as a source of objective truth. Thomas Kuhn, in particular, has had an enormous impact on ideas about science and its methods with his argument that science advances not through careful attention to the experimental method but through new ideas introduced during periods of fundamental cultural change.[37] These cultural upheavals cause paradigmatic changes in how science is viewed and thus lead to major discoveries. Kuhn, in effect, has suggested that the physical sciences, which have since Newton stood as the ultimate test of truth in the Western world, are more culturally and historically conditioned than was previously recognized.

Paralleling this intellectual controversy have been attacks on positivism that have damaged its claims, probably irreparably. By defining meaningful statements as those that have tangible referents or are statements of mathematical or formal logic, positivists believed that they could construct a form of truth that encompassed all areas of human life. But, despite herculean, and Procrustean, efforts toward this goal, the positivists could not overcome the diversities of human life and the reality of intangibles as causes of human behavior. Douglas J. Amy asserts that

> positivist methodologies continue to dominate in policy analysis, despite the fact that their intellectual foundations were undermined at least a decade ago. Positivism survives because it limits, in a way that is politically convenient, the kinds of questions that analysis can investigate. Moreover, the aura of science and objectivity that surrounds positivist policy analysis adds to the image of the policy analyst as an apolitical technocrat.[38]

Whether they have bothered to think the issues through thoroughly or not, policy analysts obviously obtain some benefit from the persistence of outmoded preconceptions about what they are doing. As is becoming increasingly apparent, however, the price being paid for this lack of perspective has been serious confusion about the proper role of the analyst in the policy process and American political culture at large.

The Analyst in the Policy Process

Before working through conceptions of the role of the policy analyst in contemporary America, it may be helpful to relate briefly the activities of the policy analyst to the complex of considerations that enter into democratic policy decisions. In broad terms, and certainly there are some who would argue for a much narrower definition, one might describe the working analyst's duties as including collection and organization of data, application of appropriate analytical techniques, clarification of the issues involved, and formulation of alternatives for resolution of a problem, with perhaps a recommendation as to the best way to go. These are important tasks, and each of them involves some judgment on the analyst's part. But the bottom line in a pluralistic society is that for the policy maker, the rational methodology of analysis constitutes only one kind of approach to a problem, and often not the most persuasive one. As Rosemarie Tong has observed, in the political process there are other, equally legitimate forms of argument than the logical-rational mode of policy analysis.[39]

The Environment of Policy Decisions

Policy makers draw on a variety of considerations in reaching decisions. While some of those lacking analytical rigor may be deplored, others make perfectly good sense from a democratic perspective. A policy maker may respond to the intensity of particular interests, as for example with the abortion issue. He or she may defer to the intuitive grasp of a situation by an experienced adviser or friend, as President Harry Truman did in moving the United States to support the creation of Israel. In other cases, programs like Head Start may have such strong emotional appeal that, regardless of findings as to their effectiveness, a policy maker will refuse to change them. Also, many policy decisions are the result of compromise among a number of officials representing different personal and political perspectives. Indeed, Douglas Yates, Jr., contends that a failure to recognize these political facets of the policy process can convert the policy analyst into a "source of rigidity in the give and take of conflict resolution."[40] Many tradeoffs and sources of influence enter into policy decisions, and policy analysis is merely one among them. Definitions of the public interest come in many sizes and shapes, and the analyst must remain aware that it is the very essence of democratic policy making to draw on a range of sources in constructing the public interest on a particular issue.

There are also a number of factors inherent in the nature of policy analysis itself that contribute toward ensuring that it will remain but one, although increasingly important, form of input into the making of pluralistic, democratic policy. Of prime importance, perhaps, are the clear elitist implications of deferring heavily to the opinions of experts. Descriptions of the physical world, whether by physical scientists or social scientists, cannot by themselves produce normative standards. No matter how skilled an individual is in an area, he or she will remain democratically incompetent to impose value positions on the public.[41] At the same time, it is important to recognize that the methodologies used by analysts carry with them necessary normative choices in terms of assumptions involved in identifying problems and goals.[42] Indeed, Laurence Tribe goes so far as to assert that policy analysis has an individualistic ethic that is utilitarian, liberal, democratic, and egalitarian.[43]

In addition to the tactical and normative considerations involved in applying a methodology to a problem, the analyst invariably suffers from more practical limitations. These revolve around money and time, as does much of life. Rarely do analysts have sufficient time to collect enough information and analyze it as thoroughly as they would wish. At times when the focus of the problem is narrow and specific and time is of the essence, as with the use of operations research during World War II, policy analysis may well determine the final decision. But in the course of the normal policy process, it will likely continue to receive heavy competition from many other directions.

The expectation, or hope, harbored by some social scientists that it is but a matter of time until the policy world conforms to the canons of logical structure is badly misplaced. The dislocations between the methods of the policy analyst and those of the politician, bureaucrat, or judge must remain because the two approaches begin from fundamentally different premises and often strive for different goals. To deal with this dichotomy constructively, the politically effective policy analyst will combine technical skill with an understanding of the political and normative contexts of the issues being considered. The chapters that follow have as a common goal the enhancement of that understanding.

The Role of the Analyst

For the policy analyst, organizational affiliation and issue orientation can be fairly closely interrelated. Generally speaking, analysts working within a public interest group (the Sierra Club) or a private interest group (the U.S. Chamber of Commerce) will evince a greater degree of activism than those operating in the middle echelons of the New York State Department of Education or the U.S. Bureau of Standards. But at times the organizational climate of even the most established agencies can transform passive analysts into advocates.

Those analysts working within the bowels of the bureaucracy tend to identify eventually with their agency's ideology, and when that agency's turf or mission is threatened, they may well be drawn into the controversies and conflicts generated in the effort to maintain agency status. In fact, these kinds of conflicts can, from the perspective of those affected, be far more intense than conflicts generated by differences over substantive issues of more general public interest.

An assumption that should form the basis for any legitimate conception of policy analysis as a profession is that the analyst is a person of professional integrity. In his study of policy analysts in the federal bureaucracy, Arnold J. Meltsner rightly concludes that integrity is a fundamental standard.

> To be politically sensitive does not mean to be insensitive to ethics or morality.... Those who are dishonest, distort their work, and deliberately lie should have no place in the analytic fraternity.[44]

Tong supports this view with her argument, drawing on discussions of professional ethics generally, that analysts should demonstrate the attributes of honesty, candor, competence, diligence, loyalty, and discretion as components of trustworthiness.[45] Although no serious student of the policy process would disagree with the merit of these qualities, discussions limited to integrity are of little more help than, say, the scouting code for the analyst dealing daily with a variety of complex issues. In a more practical vein, Robert D. Behn has suggested that doing "policy analysis well requires intellectual honesty, political creativity, a respect for a diversity of values, the ability to deflate phoniness, and some scientific rigor."[46]

At this point it is probably advisable to sound a cautionary note against the tendency of scholars to move quickly to worst-possible-case scenarios when discussing ethics and the professional policy analyst. While these hypothetical cases provide opportunities for classroom discussions, it really is difficult to see their day-to-day relevance for the working analyst. Fortunately, it is exceptionally rare that an analyst is in a position where he or she sees clients sending people to their deaths or causing widespread disease or pestilence. In these instances, one would expect an analyst, simply as a decent human being, to speak out, just as one would expect anyone aware of a serious wrong to act to correct it. Much of this kind of discussion derives from the powerful perspective offered by post hoc analysis. It is, of course, easier to point to what should have been than to make the correct decision at the time. But it is not helpful to an understanding of the policy process to be too eager to ascribe sinister or criminal motives to those who have made decisions that have had unfortunate consequences. The point is that these issues involve disputes in which reasonable persons can and do differ. That is the virtue, and sometimes the defect, of the democratic political process.

Attempts to categorize the styles and perspectives of policy analysts tend to make a basic distinction between analysts who see themselves as technicians who are not politically involved and those who take a more activist role. Both Meltsner and Hank C. Jenkins-Smith,[47] for example, see the technician as a rudimentary policy analyst type. Both also posit the more politically involved analyst as a contrasting type. They describe this second type somewhat differently, however. Jenkins-Smith, who presents his discussion in terms of organizational context, believes that issue advocates (e.g., those working for causes) and client advocates (e.g., those working for congressmen) are accurate ways of categorizing the more activist analysts. Meltsner, who limits his study to the bureaucracy and adopts a perspective drawing on the analyst's self-image, thinks of activist analysts in terms of entrepreneurs and politicians. In Meltsner's typology, the politician, the most removed from day-to-day technical analysis, possesses the instincts of a high-level political bureaucrat and is dedicated to advancing the interests of his or her supervisor or political leader. The entrepreneur, in contrast, is technically skilled but wants a greater voice in policy decisions.

Both Meltsner and Jenkins-Smith indicate that the technician posture is that most widely assumed by policy analysts. Organizationally, one would expect to find analysts with a technician orientation most numerous in the middle and lower echelons of bureaucratic hierarchies, where they have some insulation from political pressures, and, to some extent, in think tanks or academic settings. The technician simply wants to "get on with the job" and values insulation from the political as an advantage of the job. Beyond the question of personal orientation, however, is the possibility that the technician stance is a response to the policy environment. Scott and Shore assert, for example, that narrowly focused, technical studies are the kind of input that policy makers value. In their view, administrators are most receptive to succinct analysis that provides them with usable data. In this regard, the technician may simply be responding to the demands of his or her supervisors.[48] Additionally, the neutral, objective aura of expertise projected by the technician may convey an authoritative image that enhances his or her status.

The questions that emanate from the technician perspective do not in any way draw into question the analytical skills or the integrity of the analyst. They relate instead to the personal satisfaction that can be derived from such a limited perspective and to the degree to which narrowly focused analysis can be effective in the policy process. In Meltsner's view, the technician believes that he or she is objective and scientific.[49] But analysis of any kind is immersed in cultural assumptions and tactical normative judgments relative to the methodology used, and these condition the range of alternatives that can be considered in any specific study. In other words, whether they acknowledge it or not, technicians must make value judgments. Jenkins-Smith indicates that these kinds of issues are leading to increasing criticism of the technician perspective.[50] In terms of immediate effect on the policy process, one of the most important questions raised by the technician self-image rests on its apolitical claims, for as one of Meltsner's entrepreneurs argues: "Only analysts who use political considerations will do relevant and influential analysis."[51] In contrast, Scott and Shore conclude that bureaucrats are receptive to narrow, technical analysis because it enables them to implement programs more easily.

Each individual is, of course, free to choose the image that he or she wants to convey and attempt to work within. But those articulating the technician view must accept the consequences of narrowness and superficiality or be prepared to operate in an activist manner behind the technician facade that has been constructed. While the technician's work in a textbook sense may be very skilled, without more it must be politically flawed. And in the democratic policy process, that is often a fatal attribute in terms of influence. The dichotomy, to be clear, need not be between technical narrowness and a politically activist position. It seems feasible for an analyst to take great satisfaction in technical work and yet develop the awareness and interpersonal skills to make that work attractive to decision makers.

The Challenge of Activism
The closer the policy analyst becomes tied to issue advocacy, the more likely that questions will be raised about adherence to professional standards and the effect of untoward pressures on the analyst. On reflection, however, there appears to be no logical objection to the existence of professional analytical integrity and partisanship in the same unit, be it interest group, congressional committee, or administrative agency. The argument here seems reasonably straightforward. The analyst owes his or her client, from both the perspective of the analyst's standards and that of the client's need to be fully informed, the best analysis of which he or she is capable. The client, of course, then remains free to accept or reject the alternatives put forth. At this point in the literature, differences between the policy analyst and the policy maker are often stretched to raise fundamental ethical issues.

Unfortunately, moving the discussion to that of fundamental moral differences tends to obscure the essential distinctions between policy analysis and the factors involved in making political decisions. As discussed above, there is no inherent reason why the policy analyst's views should make better public policy than the opinions implemented by decision makers. The move of the Justice Department under Attorney General Edwin Meese to lessen job protections for those with acquired immune deficiency syndrome (AIDS) provides one example in this respect. There is little question that the Justice Department position ran counter to the views of many experts on AIDS, who saw minimal danger from the employment of AIDS victims. Nonetheless, in their policy position, the Justice Department exploited the degree of uncertainty involved in knowledge about transmission of the disease. The issue here is not whether the Justice decision was wise or unwise. Clearly, the Justice Department was moving toward different goals and responding to different constituencies from those influencing many experts in the field. While they may have recognized that their approach carried the risk that expert opinion might eventually have considerable weight with the courts or the electorate, they believed that they had the right to act as they did. An analyst may become so outraged by a policy decision that he or she chooses to resign, but such a decision is a personal moral act and should not be confused with the fact that there are inherent differences between policy analysis and democratic decision making.[52] To argue otherwise is to slip into the error of assuming that policy analysis is in fact an objective, scientific form of endeavor that results in unbiased truth. In a given situation, it may result in suggestions that to external observers appear far more reasonable than the public policy promulgated, but such differences are an essential characteristic of democracies. Nevertheless, most laypersons and experts could justifiably be expected to exclude astrological findings, for example, as useful policy input in any sense.

This is not to argue that the analyst should be unconcerned about values in his or her work. Quite the contrary. Understanding and examining the various normative issues involved in a problem are the most difficult tasks that an analyst faces in the attempt to provide really useful material for the policy process. We examine the intricacies involved in integrating normative perspectives into analysis in detail later. But here it is important to note that the retreat into claims of objectivity and science is too easy an approach to invariably complex policy issues. Policy analysis that moves beyond the assertions of objectivity and efficiency is one route toward analysis that speaks more comprehensively to social concerns.

Because policy analysts have not been able to influence the policy process to a great extent, some have urged a greater degree of advocacy on the part of the analyst.[53] While advocacy in itself is a perfectly legitimate form of activity for the analyst, as for most other citizens, it may tempt him or her to try to gain advantage through the manipulation of data and findings. That some should succumb to this temptation is not surprising in view of the emotions and reputations that may be at stake. Even the natural sciences, where the standards of research are perhaps more rigorous (but the rewards far more prestigious and profitable), have experienced notorious cases of fudged data and findings. The ramifications of such behavior for a scientist or policy analyst can be disastrous for the individual personally and damaging to the profession involved.

In a pluralistic society, it is simply expecting too much for analysis to go unchallenged. Meltsner, who has served as editor of *Policy Analysis,* emphasizes that studies of policy issues are vulnerable to a wide range of criticisms.

Analysts and researchers are shot down for wrong assumptions, for too circumscribed or biased a view of the problem, for bad research design, for faulty and misleading statistics, for lack of causal connection between hypotheses and findings, for simpleminded hypotheses, and for alternatives involving conflicting objectives.[54]

Such attacks do their share to heighten controversy over public policy issues, but they, too, are part of the process. The introduction of *deliberately* distorted analyses into the cause of partisanship, however, converts policy analysis from an approach that can make very real contributions to clarifying issues and suggesting alternatives into simply another manipulative tactic in the already confused arena of interest-group politics. Although policy analysis has not provided the steady guide to public policy that many have hoped, it clearly has been an asset to that process, and it is a happy circumstance that standards of integrity have stood as the overriding rule.

Policy analysts have the capability to continue to provide useful input to the policy process in an era when American society increasingly faces problems so complex in substance that they are beyond the layperson's comprehension and yet so pervasive that they touch everyone's fundamental beliefs. Advanced means for controlling the reproductive process through genetic planning, improvement of life-sustaining technology for severely handicapped newborn infants and the comatose elderly, and the development of increasingly sophisticated devices for monitoring every moment and movement of one's privacy are but a few of the inevitable changes that must raise serious questions for policy makers. No doubt new methodologies and techniques will also be devised to improve analytical prowess. But more important to the status of policy analysis will be the degree to which its practitioners are able to combine technical skills with a certain humility about their use, a mature sense of the vicissitudes of politics, and a recognition of the necessity and difficulty of reconciling normative concerns.

Notes

1. Russell L. Hanson, *The Democratic Imagination in America* (Princeton: Princeton University Press, 1985), 224.

2. William Graham Sumner, *Essays of William Graham Sumner*, ed. Albert Galloway Keller and Maurice R. Davie (New Haven: Yale University Press, 1934), 1:6.

3. Robert A. Scott and Arnold R. Shore, *Why Sociology Does Not Apply* (New York: Elsevier, 1979), 9, 108.

4. Richard J. Bernstein, *John Dewey* (New York: Washington Square Press, 1966), 1.

5. John Dewey, *The Public and Its Problems* (Chicago: Gateway Books, 1946 [1927]).

6. Arthur F. Bentley, *The Process of Government* (Evanston, Ill.: Principia Press of Illinois, 1949 [1908]), 172.

7. Ibid., 177.

8. Ibid., 208.

9. From *Interpretations of Legal History* (1923), 1, quoted in Fred H. Cahill, *Judicial Legislation* (New York: Ronald Press, 1952), 73.

10. Scott and Shore, *Why Sociology*, 121.

11. Mary O. Furner, *Advocacy and Objectivity* (Lexington, Ky.: University Press of Kentucky, 1975).

12. Kenneth P. Davis, *FDR: The New Deal Years, 1933–1937* (New York: Random House, 1986), 236–37.

13. Ibid., 234–36, 675.

14. Jurgen Schmandt and James Everett Katz, "The Scientific State: A Theory with Hypotheses," *Science, Technology, and Human Values,* Winter 1986, 40–52.

15. Ibid., 49.

16. Ibid., 48.

17. Ibid., 45.

18. Michel Crozier, *The Trouble With America* (Berkeley: University of California Press, 1984), 48–49.

19. Aaron Wildavsky, "Rescuing Policy Analysis from PPBS" in *Public Expenditures and Policy Analysis,* ed. Robert H. Haveman and Julius Margolis (Chicago: Rand McNally, 1970), 461–81.

20. See Paul F. Lazarsfeld, Jeffrey G. Reitz, Ann K. Pasanella, *An Introduction to Applied Sociology* (New York: Elsevier, 1975) .

21. David Easton, "The New Revolution in Political Science," *American Political Science Review* 63 (December 1969): 1051–61.

22. Harold D. Lasswell, "The Policy Orientation" in *The Policy Sciences,* ed. Daniel Lerner and Harold D. Lasswell (Stanford: Stanford University Press, 1951), 3–15.

23. Yehezkel Dror, "Policy Analysts: A New Professional Role in Government Service," *Public Administration Review* 27 (September 1967): 197–203.

24. John P. Crecine, ed., *The New Educational Programs in Public Policy* (Greenwich, Conn.: JAI Press, 1982), 21, n. 1; Joel L. Fleishman, "The Creation of a Profession" in *What Role for Government?* ed. Richard J. Zeckhauser and Derek Leebaert (Durham, N.C.: Duke University Press, 1983), 324–26.

25. Frank Fischer, "Policy Expertise and the 'New Class': A Critique of the Neoconservative Thesis" in *Confronting Values in Policy Analysis,* ed. Frank Fischer and John Forester (Newbury Park, Calif.: Sage, 1987), 103.

26. Crozier, *Trouble With America*, 51.

27. Daniel P. Moynihan, *Maximum Feasible Misunderstanding* (New York: Free Press, 1970), 35–36.

28. Frances Fox Piven and Richard A. Cloward, *Regulating the Poor* (New York: Vintage, 1972), 248–49, n. 1.

29. Carol Hirschon Weiss, "Evaluating Social Programs: What Have We Learned?" *Society* 25 (November-December 1987): 41.

30. Edward Banfield, *The Unheavenly City* (Boston: Little, Brown, 1970). Banfield revised this work in 1974.

31. Fischer, "Policy Expertise," 104–5.

32. Henry J. Aaron, *Politics and the Professors* (Washington, D.C.: Brookings Institution, 1978), 158–59; Weiss, "Evaluating Social Programs," 41–42.

33. David B. Truman, *The Governmental Process* (New York: Knopf, 1951).

34. Charles E. Lindblom, "The Science of 'Muddling Through,'" *Public Administration Review* 19 (Spring 1959): 79–88.

35. Ibid., 85.

36. Ibid., 86.

37. Thomas S. Kuhn, *The Structure of Scientific Revolutions*, 2d ed. (Chicago: University of Chicago Press, 1970); see also Yehezkel Dror, "On Becoming More of a Policy Scientist," *Policy Studies Review* 4 (August 1984): 15.

38. Douglas J. Amy, "Toward a Post-Positivist Policy Analysis," *Policy Studies Journal* 13 (September 1984): 210–11.

39. Rosemarie Tong, *Ethics in Public Policy* (Englewood Cliffs, N.J.: Prentice-Hall, 1986), 124–25.

40. Douglas Yates, Jr., *The Politics of Management* (San Francisco: Jossey-Bass, 1985), 110.

41. Scott and Shore, *Why Sociology*, 142, 144.

42. Ibid., 138–43; Charles E. Lindblom, *The Policy-Making Process*, 2d ed. (Englewood Cliffs, N.J.: Prentice-Hall, 1980), 22–25.

43. Laurence Tribe, "Policy Science: Analysis or Ideology?" *Philosophy and Public Affairs* 2 (Fall 1972): 66–110.

44. Arnold J. Meltsner, *Policy Analysts in the Bureaucracy* (Berkeley: University of California Press, 1976), 282.

45. Tong, *Ethics*, 92.

46. Robert D. Behn, "Policy Analysts, Clients, and Social Scientists," *Journal of Policy Analysis and Management* 4 (Spring 1985): 430.

47. Hank C. Jenkins-Smith, "Professional Roles for Policy Analysts: A

Critical Assessment," *Journal of Policy Analysis and Management* 2 (Fall 1982): 88–100.

48. Scott and Shore, *Why Sociology,* 188–89.

49. Meltsner, *Policy Analysts,* 23.

50. Jenkins-Smith, "Professional Roles," 93.

51. Meltsner, *Policy Analysts,* 43.

52. On this point generally, see Peter W. House and Roger D. Shull, *Rush to Policy* (New Brunswick, N.J.: Transaction, 1988), 131.

53. J.M.B. Fraatz, "Policy Analysts as Advocates," *Journal of Policy Analysis and Management* 1 (Winter 1982): 273–76.

54. Meltsner, *Policy Analysts,* 274.

CHAPTER 2

Rationality and Decision Making

Policy Analysis: A Thumbnail Sketch

This chapter examines policy analysts as actors in the policy process. In particular, it discusses the normative factors that influence the techniques often used by analysts and that emerge as important determinants of decision making in the policy process. Values in both areas serve as important contextual constraints on the use of analytical findings. The kind of policy analysis performed by working analysts might be termed prescriptive in that ① it normally results in recommendations of some sort. Other forms of policy analysis focus on studying the policy process and are not geared toward ② making specific recommendations. Some studies, for example, trace proposals through the various stages of the policy process. Others examine the origins and effects of policies in particular areas. Whether or not they gener-③ ate recommendations, all three approaches to policy analysis share common characteristics. They strive to improve government decisions and provide information that can be used to enhance the quality of life, and they proceed on the assumption that one can analytically study policies, their causes, and their consequences. Policy analysis that produces recommendations (prescriptive analysis) raises the most interesting and practical questions about how values affect analysis and how analysis, in turn, affects policy decisions.

Since the early efforts of the great philosophical system builders of the seventeenth century, students of society have been attracted by the possibility of constructing models of social behavior that have the rigor and predictive power of those in the physical sciences. These attempts persist, and it is easy for the student to confuse the meanings of *science* as used in the physical sciences with its often rather loose and diverse use in the social sciences. Science has had tremendous status in the Western world, and appropriation of that label has been seen as a way of providing legitimacy to a number of different fields of activity.

In the seventeenth and eighteenth centuries, claims were made that a truly scientific model of society was possible. Usually, these models were based on the principles of deductive reasoning. Through an incisive argument, as yet essentially unanswered, David Hume discredited those ambitious notions. Hume asserted that only in the constructs of mathematics and logic can necessary relationships be established by deductive reason. In society and the physical world, cause-and-effect relationships are only inferences drawn from observing the high correlation of certain events. One cannot *prove* that a second event is caused by the first. Finally, Hume pointed out that what had been seen as universal rational truths, such as the value of private property or individual liberty, were in fact only conventions that societies had found useful or agreeable. In short, deductive reason utilizing logically necessary relationships could not provide the basis for a science of society.

In the aftermath of Hume's attack, thinkers continued to argue, on other grounds, that a scientific model of society was possible. In the nineteenth century, Charles Darwin's evolutionary ideas were appropriated as a basis for a science of society. In the twentieth century, an important movement encouraging the idea of a science of society was logical positivism. As noted in the preceding chapter, positivists tried to define all meaningful sentences as either representations of empirical phenomena or analytical statements. One of this school's leading proponents, A.J. Ayer, later conceded that this is not possible and was misguided.[1] Nonetheless, social scientists became heavily influenced by the idea that their disciplines could become more scientific by eliminating metaphysical values and assumptions and dealing directly with human behavior. Because of the insistence by logical positivists and social scientists on the need for tangible referents, their analyses tended to be confined to empirical description. When applied to policy analysis, this orientation can favor the immediately useful in policy outcomes.

Yet the philosophical basis for a narrow analytical focus that precluded the incorporation of intangibles such as perceptions and values was rapidly eroding. Taking a different perspective on the scientific enterprise, Karl Popper, an eminent philosopher of science, maintained that no scientific conclusions can be certain. They have a tentative validity that lasts only until they are found deficient in some manner. In fact, to be scientific, a statement or hypothesis must be falsifiable. If Popper's position is sound, narrowing the focus of social science to achieve a certainty believed to exist in the physical sciences is self-defeating. Popper's ideas on the scientific method also address the limitations of schools of social science that attempt to exclude values from their studies. Addressing the inductive approach to scientific research, Popper has demonstrated that, before any data collection can start, the researcher must have some idea of where and how to begin.[2] In the social sciences, this speaks directly to the fact that research must begin with assumptions about what is worth investigating. Carried far enough back, this line of reasoning must lead one to the researcher's basic value assumptions and interests.

As long as human dignity and meaning exist as important values, social science cannot achieve the rigor of the physical sciences because it is impossible to separate human beliefs from the context and process of analysis. Normative assumptions as to the value of health, long life, security, or wealth permeate human endeavors. The alternative would be to treat human beings simply as guinea pigs and to utilize them as scientific objects, a situation that has been approached by some regimes but one that is totally antithetical to democratic values. Essentially, when science is applied as a label to the pursuit of policy analysis, what is being described is the careful accumulation of data, rigorous study of possible interpretations and alternatives, and the articulation of reasons for the recommended course of action. None of this can be objective in the sense in which that term describes, for example, scientists' search for material capable of superconductivity, because it cannot be removed from the values of the particular analyst. Nonetheless, policy analysis remains an exceedingly important approach to the policy process, and it can be even more significant with careful attention to its involvement with social and personal values.

Today, many students of policy analysis agree that it is important to consider values in the process of policy analysis. While lip service to the importance of values is freely given, however, there is normally little discussion about how normative considerations are to be made part of the analytical process. In fact, analysts' findings are still often described as "objective." Failure to consider broader societal values, the complexities of the policy process itself, and the uncertainties of the political context constrict even further the viewpoint provided on policy analysis.

This chapter attempts to integrate a normative viewpoint into the consideration of policy analysis. It examines some important techniques of policy analysis, values underlying these techniques, and the use of analysis by decision makers. In a broader context, the role of policy analysts in the policy process and the critical—and sometimes ignored—impact of values on that process are also considered.

Ideology and Policy Analysis

In a pluralistic society such as the United States, variety in belief systems is a natural consequence of differences in backgrounds and aspirations. To the extent that they provide reasonably comprehensive rationales for expectations about how government should act, belief systems can be said to constitute ideologies. Although they may be neither rational in structure nor cognitively salient, ideological beliefs are especially influential normative frameworks for both policy analysts and decision makers. Here, welfare liberalism, utilitarianism, social conservatism, and support for the institutional status quo are examined as ideologies that in the past several decades have significantly influenced many of those who have been active in the policy process. These belief systems can be fairly directly linked to policy positions, in contrast to the more amorphous and general ideological views held by the electorate.

Dewey and Welfare Liberalism

Dewey's ideas have provided the most comprehensive philosophical support for welfare liberalism, an ideology supporting an activist government and social reform through scientific analysis. Dewey was an early advocate of the idea of a "positive state" that would take responsibility for acting to redress social grievances. For him, this was the essence of modern liberalism. At one point he wrote,

> The majority who call themselves liberals today are committed to the principle that organized society must use its powers to establish the conditions under which the mass of individuals can possess actual as distinct from merely legal liberty. They define their liberalism in the concrete in the terms of a program of measures moving toward this end. They believe that a conception of the state which limits the activities of the latter to keeping order as between individuals and to securing redress for one person when another person infringes the liberty existing law has given him, is in effect simply a justification of the brutalities and inequities of the existing order.[3]

In urging a pragmatic approach to dealing with social problems, Dewey emphasized the importance of results—what worked best was best. Government should try different policies in the spirit of working hypotheses for approaching solutions to problems.

The need to adopt the experimental method in applying "organized intelligence" to the cause of social reform was a consistent theme throughout Dewey's extensive writings. He saw this as the means by which government could become more "scientific" in the formulation of policy Scientists and experts from other fields would provide data for policy makers.

> Their expertness is not shown in framing and executing policies, but in discovering and making known the facts upon which the former depend. They are technical experts in the sense that scientific investigators and artists manifest expertise.[4]

In his efforts to have government apply organized intelligence to social problems, Dewey seemed to be calling for the creation of a profession much like policy analysis. Harold Lasswell was later to note the importance of Dewey in this respect with his comment that the policy sciences "are a contemporary adaptation of the general approach to public policy that was recommended by John Dewey and his colleagues in the development of American pragmatism."[5]

Dewey was a spokesman for the welfare liberal ideology of social reform through government's social intervention, a perspective that has formed the presuppositions of many policy analysts. Critics of Dewey have pointed out that his pragmatic approach provided strong support for analysis of social problems but few guidelines as to what constituted acceptable solutions. Analysts whose work is informed by welfare liberalism may discover that careful analysis of issues cannot overcome the normative power of competing ideological positions held by decision makers. In these instances, the practical use of their recommendations will be minimal.

Utilitarianism

A bias toward the value of efficiency is inherent in the methods of policy analysis, and utilitarianism has been the ideological position most forthrightly incorporating this standard as a central value. Laurence H. Tribe, following the analysis of John Rawls, has argued that the heavy reliance of policy analysis on economic concepts and methods has fostered a "wants" orientation toward public choices, in which "wants" are defined simply as what individuals happen to desire.[6] Alternatives are weighted in terms of self-interest, usually measured in monetary terms. Public policies that do well by this standard are deemed to be efficient and therefore "good." Tribe contends that public policy should be based on values and principles larger than quantifiable costs and benefits, and his critique focuses on one of the ironies, and limitations, of policy analysis performed within a utilitarian framework. This approach incorporates efficiency as a basic value while maintaining a posture of being "value free."

Any methodology undertaken in social analysis will have value judgments within it. Policy analysis from utilitarian assumptions, however, carries the ever-present danger that values unacceptable to the public will be surreptitiously promoted under the guise of "objective" analysis. Utilitarianism has provided firm ideological support for many of the methods of policy analysis, but, unlike Dewey's pragmatic welfare liberalism, it does not necessarily promote social reform by activist government. In fact, at least one important American school of utilitarian thought supports limited government and greater market freedom for private activity as the most efficient form of public policy.

The basic belief of utilitarianism is that laws, customs, and institutions should be evaluated in terms of their social utility. Jeremy Bentham, the intellectual father of utilitarianism, declared that

> by the principle of utility is meant that principle which approves or disapproves of every action whatsoever, according to the tendency which it appears to have to augment or diminish the happiness of the party whose interest is in question.... I say of every action whatsoever; and therefore not only of every action of a private individual, but of every measure of government.[7]

From this perspective, the idea of human good becomes equated with preference. The guiding criterion for policy is the greatest good for society, quantitatively defined. But contemporary utilitarians, primarily economists and theorists of public choice, like Bentham, still have no principle for distributing this social good according to manifest principles of equity. "One dollar, one vote" is not on the face of it an acceptable principle.

The basic difficulty with both Dewey's liberalism and utilitarianism is that public policy is left without any firm normative foundations on which to act. That is, if the focus of decision makers is on making things better for people through application of the pragmatic or utilitarian approach, it remains unclear what level of wants deserves attention. In a pluralistic society, can utilitarianism establish a consensual hierarchy of wants? Which is more important, a policy that establishes a universal legal right to a decent minimum of health care (national health insurance) or one that contains growing public health-care costs? How are the opposed values of environmental integrity and full employment to be reconciled? The effort to satisfy people's wants can also deflect attention away from the processes by which decisions are made. If an authoritarian government is most efficient (*reductio ad absurdum*), then is not that the best form of government? Mussolini, after all, made the trains run on time.

Social Conservatism

In recent years, social conservatism has emerged as an ideology with substantive, if somewhat amorphous, content and with implications for public policy. With its concern for family and religious values, this ideology has popular appeal and provides the background for opposition to abortion, support for school prayer, proposals for aid to parochial schools, and similar positions. Historically, in America social analysis has claimed to provide value-free rationales for social reform. The social conservatives, however, make no pretensions of being without value positions and have shown flexibility in applying analytical techniques in support of their policy proposals. Charles Murray's *Losing Ground,* which extensively criticizes liberal welfare policies, is an example of this approach.[8]

Institutional Status Quo Orientation

To the extent that policy analysts are part of an ongoing government agency, they may become so closely tied to their agency's programs that their analyses will not suggest radical changes from the status quo. Anthony Downs notes the tendency for bureaucrats to adopt the values of their agency and to come to defend that agency's "turf."[9] Meltsner applies this to policy analysts; he notes that the analyst "cannot escape the preferences of his organization; and soon, rather than remaining a skeptical generalist, he, like other bureaucrats, becomes a defender of the faith."[10]

Some contend that policy analysts from outside an agency can avoid a status quo orientation and have some policy impact. Regulatory reform in the federal government under Ronald Reagan has been used as an example: Lawrence M. Mead concludes that "precisely because the outsiders were more academic, closer to the economic paradigm of the free market [as compared with the analysts in the bureaucracy], their thinking was *more* effective in broad policy terms, not less."[11] Getting outside the status quo can, at least on occasion, actually *increase* the effectiveness of policy analysts—if their views are closer to those of powerful clients, such as the President, than are the perspectives of bureaucratically situated analysts.

Non-efficiency-based Values

One common value underlying policy analysis, as already mentioned, is economic efficiency, a component of what is termed "the politics of interest" in chapter 3. Other values also could be taken into account by the analyst. These make the task of providing advice to clients even more complex for policy analysts, as these are frequently "soft" values that cannot readily be quantified. What value, for example, should be placed on human life, the beauty of a redwood forest, or preservation of the whale?

Charles Anderson argues that authority and justice must also be recognized as standards by which public policy is measured. He asserts that authority is "a necessary characteristic of any legitimate policy decision."[12] If a decision cannot be demonstrated to be a rightful exercise of government power, it is simply an act of coercion or domination. In short, "good reasons have to be given for regarding a problem or project as appropriately the subject of public action."[13] With regard to the dimension of justice, the policy analyst should begin with treating like cases alike and dissimilar cases differently. The policy analyst who is sensitive to normative concerns should recognize that "any policy evaluation must include a justification of the categories of universal or differential treatment to be established."[14] For example, treating two individuals in essentially similar situations differently by providing an advantage to one or the other must be defensible. Anderson, then, contends that efficiency alone is not sufficient justification for a policy recommendation by an analyst. Authority and justice must also be considered, and as the following chapter indicates, principles of justice, in particular, may be various.

The next chapter discusses in detail two separate wellsprings for values—interest and conscience, or the utilitarian perspective vs. the deontological or Kantian. Policy analytic techniques are dominated by efficiency-based utilitarian criteria. The second set of values, which utilizes ideas such as equality, justice, the moral worth of each individual, and the common good, and is clearly metaphysical and transcendent in nature, generally receives little consideration in the application of analytical techniques. But, as chapter 3 illustrates, ethicists have argued that this need not and *should not* be the case and have shown how different values can be tied into policy analysis.

How Policy Analysis Is Used

Recent studies, examined below, indicate that one must distinguish at least two kinds of use of policy analysis: instrumental and enlightenment. While instrumental use is the most common way in which analysis is expected to have an impact, such expectations are frequently disappointed.

As reported by Grover Starling, interviews with 204 policy makers indicated a generally positive attitude toward policy analysis. Nevertheless, only 13 percent could name as many as five to ten instances of having used policy analyses, whereas 44 percent reported explicitly disregarding such information. Starling also notes that a 1976 General Accounting Office (GAO) study found that 30 percent of federal units questioned said that policy analysis had accomplished nothing; 30 percent indicated some use of it; 40 percent suggested that it may have had an impact, but that sorting out the independent effects of policy analysis as compared with other inputs was very difficult.[15]

Michael Quinn Patton's examination of twenty evaluations of federal programs also suggests little independent impact of analytical research on decision making. The effects tended to be a reinforcement of decision makers' preexisting views or the filling in of a few gaps in their knowledge. Overall, research seems to reduce uncertainty in decision situations. Patton concludes that utilization "is a diffuse and gradual process of reducing decision-makers' uncertainty within an existing social context."[16]

David Whiteman explored congressional committees' use of Office of Technology Assessment (OTA) research. He found that use of information depended on the situation. Substantive impacts (i.e., helping committees outline a legislative position) occurred in the early stages of committee work. In later stages, the use was "strategic" (justifying, confirming, reinforcing an already preferred position). Overall, strategic use was more common.[17] Peter House and Roger Shull, two practitioners of policy analysis, support these findings. Using a series of case studies as a data base, they conclude that "possibly the single most important lesson to be learned ... is that no sophisticated or formal decision technique ... was really used in these decision processes in the sense ... intended."[18]

There is a second, "sloppier," way in which analysis has an effect. Robert F. Rich's summary of agencies' use of a series of National Opinion Research Center (NORC) surveys of public opinion is somewhat more encouraging. He finds two distinct patterns of use. First, information from research filters upward in a bureaucracy and is used to help solve very specific problems. Then, later on, those higher in an agency may use these results to formulate broader policy ideas that are transmitted downward to lower levels to help structure future policy choices. His essay points toward a more diffuse impact of policy analysis.[19]

Carol Weiss suggests that policy analysis may be used more for "enlightenment" than for instrumental purposes, although these need *not* be mutually exclusive. She argues that clients of policy analysts may be less interested in analysis as a tool to arrive at solutions than as a means of orienting themselves toward problems. She observes of clients:

> They use research to help them think about issues and define the problematics of a situation, to gain new ideas and new perspectives. They use research to help *formulate* problems and to set the agenda for future policy actions. And much of this is not deliberate, direct, and targeted, but a result of long-term percolation of social science concepts, theories, and findings into the climate of informed opinion.[20]

Indeed, policy makers may not even be aware of where their ideas originate. They absorb bits and pieces of information from different sources—with policy analysis being one of these. Weiss refers to this diffuse use as "enlightenment."

A study of 155 mental health decision makers in the federal government indicated the possible enlightenment use of fifty research reports, even if there was little instrumental use of findings. Two distinct factors increase the odds of this diffuse use: a "truth" test and a "utility" test. The former refers to the quality of the research *and* to its conformity to clients' previous understandings, values, and experience. The latter refers to the ability of the research to help solve problems *and* to challenge the status quo. That is, if there is an interesting twist to the research that can help reorient thinking about a problem and that research challenges dominant views, the findings can assist in redefining the original problem—even if specific recommendations are not used.[21]

In summary, instrumental use of policy analysis is not as widespread as analysts would like; however, there is a more diffuse use of policy analysis, which can be significant. This use for "enlightenment" is often underplayed in the literature on utilization of policy analysis. Its existence, though, should be taken into account by the policy analyst. If the analyst cannot easily shape a specific policy, his or her findings may still have an impact on the broader policy agenda, a not insignificant contribution.

Policy Analysis: Techniques, Values, and Effects

The tools available to policy analysts seem impressive. In this section, we examine four of them: cost-benefit analysis, decision-tree methods, simulations and models, and experiments. This scarcely exhausts the supply; other approaches include an array of forecasting techniques (e.g., Delphi, linear programming, risk assessment, program evaluation review technique [PERT], and game theory.)

No agreement exists as to what discipline provides the most valid foundation for policy analysis, but in practice the methods and assumptions of economics are central. Meltsner, for instance, finds that a plurality of federal policy analysts have the greater part of their professional training in economics.[22] And, as the preceding chapter makes clear, there are historical and theoretical reasons for the influence of economics.

Cost-Benefit Analysis

One of the most basic methods of policy analysis is cost-benefit analysis. Its essence is deceptively simple: One adds up the costs of a program, then its benefits. Next, costs are subtracted from benefits. If several options are being considered, the one with the greatest *net* benefit should be selected. This axiom is referred to as the Fundamental Rule of cost-benefit analysis.

A study examining the effects of helicopter surveillance patrols on burglary rates in high-crime areas illustrates the essential elements of cost-benefit analysis.[23] Adding patrol cars to such areas has no apparent impact; however, some believe that helicopters, which provide law enforcement officers with greater ability to see wrongful acts, might have a more significant impact on crime. The study indicates a reduction of crime rates with the introduction of helicopter patrols. The relevant question then becomes whether the reduction in crime is worth the program cost. Table 1 (page 46) summarizes the basic data.

On a cost-per-day basis, helicopter patrols expended $126; benefits amounted to $333 per day (cost of burglaries during no-helicopter patrol minus cost of burglaries committed during helicopter patrol). The resulting ratio of benefits to costs was 2.6:1, indicating that, under the logic of the Fundamental Rule, the program was justified.

As has been noted, there are a number of difficulties with this method. Some are obvious, such as the problem of putting dollar figures on intangibles like quality of life, value of a human life, or the benefits of beauty,[24] although these are often assessed indirectly; for example, a value for human life can be calculated from the rate of awards in wrongful death cases that go to trial. That the valuation of life remains problematic is clear from a comparison of government assumptions about the dollar benefits accruing when a life is saved. One cataloging of the value of a life shows that the variation across agencies is enormous, from $5 million at the Occupational Safety and Health Administration to $475,000 by the Environmental Protection Agency.[25] In the example above, what is the cost to residents of the additional noise likely to be generated by helicopter patrols? This is not an easy question to answer in dollar-and-cent terms, even though studies have been carried out with surrogate prices in cases in which no market price exists for purposes of estimate.

Table 1. Helicopter Patrol Cost-Benefit Analysis

	Daily
Cost of program	$126
Cost of burglaries during no-helicopter patrol periods	$494
Cost of burglaries during helicopter patrol periods	$161
Benefits	$333
Benefit to cost ratio	333/126 = 2.6

Another clear obstacle to the use of quantitative measures is the uncertainty often associated with a social problem. More systematic treatment can be given to known than to unknown probabilities. It is not always clear what the facts really are; costs and benefits calculated under conditions in which probabilities are not known will surely not be as reliable as desired. Aaron Wildavsky observes that "the cost-benefit analyst must learn to live with uncertainty, for he can never know whether all relevant objectives have been included and what changes may occur in policy and in technology."[26] This is not a counsel of despair but an admonition of the need to be sensitive to uncertainty.

Also, the future can be an imponderable complicating the cost-benefit calculations of the analyst. In theory, through discounting, one can incorporate the future into cost-benefit analysis. In practice, important questions remain. First, and most apparent, the future is opaque and not easily predictable, hence, there is often built-in uncertainty in considering the future. Second, consequences, in actual practice, are often not seriously weighted. Two examples illustrate these problems.

In the private sector, weighing costs and benefits tends currently to be tied to short-term thinking. A "bottom line" orientation that has focused on the importance of immediate profits has relegated basic research and capital investment to lower priorities. This appears to be one reason for the competitive success of Japanese firms against their American counterparts. Many of the former have a future orientation and are willing to forego present profits for longer-term profits. In the semiconductor industry, for instance, American firms have seen their share of the market drop markedly as the Japanese attention to long-term planning and investment has resulted in sophisticated products and a coordinated market strategy. American industry is only beginning to recognize that maintenance of a competitive position in the world economy requires planning that employs a much longer time horizon than that based on investors' demands for short-term profitability. What is at stake here, however, may be different discount rates, as between the United States and Japan, whether explicit or implicit, that draw on cultural differences.

In recent years, Florida has also felt the ill effects of a cost-benefit perspective that was not made amenable to long-term planning. Beginning in the 1950s, the state began to encourage the elderly to retire there, and the influx of retirees increased dramatically. For several decades, the benefits were enormous in terms of cash flows into the state from pensions and other kinds of support. Now, however, lengthened life spans have begun to place serious burdens on the state budget. With the lowest per capita spending on social services in the nation and the fewest nursing homes per capita, Florida must consider how to provide for an elderly population, of which almost 200,000 are already over eighty-five years of age. If public officials had carefully calculated the benefit-cost ratio for attracting the elderly to Florida, it would have been apparent that this policy was eventually going to impose tremendous costs on the state budget and the state's taxpayers. But the conclusions of cost-benefit analysis over time (often accomplished through discounting) would have fared poorly in the face of immediate economic and political considerations. Equally important, a more sophisticated calculation of costs and benefits would probably have brought basic American values into play. Despite the difficulties and costs involved, Americans remain acutely sensitive to the needs of the elderly. The pressures building on Florida are one reflection of this attitude; President Reagan's difficulties in revamping the Social Security System were another. These problems are not inherent in the cost-benefit approach but in the choice of the discount rate, which is ultimately determined by the political community, not the analyst.

Edith Stokey and Richard Zeckhauser, authors of one of the most widely used texts on analytical methods, assert that their bias in public policy is toward the well-being of individuals. In their view, "The objective of public policy ... should be to promote the welfare of society. Moreover, the welfare of society depends wholly on the welfare of individuals; it's people that count."[27] Superficially, this appears to be an incontestable position, but as the examples cited above demonstrate, the present and future needs of individuals are difficult to assess in their nature or their magnitude. When one includes the needs of future generations, the task of promoting human welfare becomes even more problematical. Edmund Burke, almost two hundred years ago, spoke to this very point with his often quoted description of the proper way of conceiving of the social contract between the state and its constituents: "As the ends of such a partnership cannot be obtained in many generations, it becomes a partnership not only between those who are living, but between those who are living, those who are dead, and those who are to be born."[28]

Individuals, it is true, count for a great deal, but the analyst must be aware that the techniques that he or she is using speak to an immediate set of conditions that have to be placed in their proper cultural context if the needs of the individual as a fully socialized human being are to be considered adequately. Those concerned about the competitive position of the American economy in the world, parents concerned about the health of their children and grandchildren, and families concerned about the treatment of their elder members raise a host of complex and often conflicting value considerations for any policy maker trying to work with problems in these areas.

With its emphasis on measurement and tangible factors, the cost-benefit form of analysis has enjoyed wide popularity with policy analysts. Yet these characteristics can also be viewed as limitations of this approach in the area of public policy. In some ways, the use of cost-benefit analysis can be a hindrance to long-range planning or commitment. This shortcoming stems as much from its insistence on quantifiable measures as on its inherently incremental bias. The cost-benefit approach used in the area of public policy usually stresses costs over benefits. One widely conceded reason for this is that many public programs—in areas such as health, education, and environmental protection—produce intangible benefits that are not quantifiable, while their dollar costs are readily calculated. But the cost-benefit approach is politically debilitating in another, less widely recognized sense, for it tends to saddle leaders with the onus of costs when their actions may have averted major disasters. Citizens can feel the pinch of the costs of public measures designed to prevent serious misfortunes, such as a natural disaster, enemy attack, or economic depression, but they may experience no noticeable benefits if the measures taken are successful. In these instances, leaders may in effect be punished by the voters for their foresight. At the same time, careful quantitative analysis of social problems remains an especially useful approach, and knowledgeable and responsible public leaders would be well advised to consider its findings.

Basic values are built into the cost-benefit method despite its surface appearance as an objective, value-free technique. The Fundamental Rule demands that the most *efficient* alternative be selected. Maximization of goods or services in quantifiable terms, usually dollars, guides decisions under cost-benefit analysis. The many factors involved in the *process* by which decisions are made are deemphasized. There is little "independent concern for the *procedures* whereby those outcomes are produced or for the *history* out of which they evolve."[29] By deemphasizing these factors, utilitarian values tend to crowd out other concerns. Slighted in the process may be such values as equity or the welfare of unborn generations. Cost-benefit analysis is exceptionally valuable for clarifying and arranging alternative ways of approaching problems, but by no stretch of the imagination can it be considered "value free."

Decision Analysis

Decision analysis is used when "decisions must be undertaken sequentially and where uncertainty is a critical element."[30] One common technique used under these conditions is the decision tree. The choice between the cost per month of purchasing a new car as compared with the purchase of a used car provides a simple example of this approach (see figure 1, page 50).

There is one *decision node* (courses of action open to the decision maker); two *chance nodes* (the uncertain events with their possible outcomes)—cost per month associated with purchase of a used (*a*) versus a new (*b*) car; *probabilities* (associated with each outcome); and *payoffs*, the consequences of each possible combination of choice and chance. The Expected Monetary Value (EMV) of buying a used car (EMV/*a*) is the average of the sum of each choice multiplied by the odds of the different choices. Simply, for a used car in this case, EMV/a = .5(1000) + .5(200) = $600. For a new car, EMV/$b$ = .1(800) + .9 (400)= $440. The better choice, then, would be to purchase a new car, since the expected monetary value ($440)—in this case, cost—is *less* than that of acquiring a used car ($600 per month).

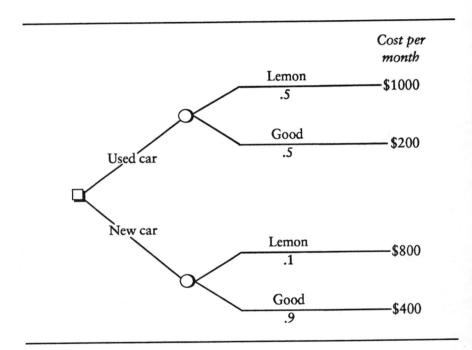

Figure 1. Decision Tree for Purchasing a Car

One immediate question about this technique is the set of quantitative assumptions undergirding each decision choice. Probability estimates and the costs associated with the array of choices are straightforward in the example above, but decision trees are often constructed when there is considerable uncertainty about root assumptions. In complex situations, branches representing various choices, or decisions, can be added at a geometric rate, making the final result dependent on a heavy amount of estimating. Susan Welch and John C. Comer say that "decision tree analysis seems more a useful heuristic device than a yardstick by which a final decision should be measured. Past experience with decision trees shows that failure rates of systems and other risks are often severely underestimated, thus making the whole payoff calculation pure fantasy."[31]

Related to these operational problems is the fact that it is not always easy to identify all relevant "branches" of the decision tree; some alternatives may simply be ignored, especially in complex situations. The Rasmussen Reactor Safety Study, for example, utilizing event-tree analysis and fault-tree analysis, methods similar to the decision-tree approach, cost $4 million over three years. Yet despite the thoroughness with which the study was conducted, within a short time after its completion it was subjected to numerous criticisms that exposed flaws in its methodology and its assumptions, indicating, again, the need for any analyst to retain a critical posture in the application of analytical techniques.[32]

Values underlying the decision-tree method parallel those of cost-benefit analysis. The approach is outcome oriented and hence reflects utilitarian values. While this tool is, on its face, more future oriented than cost-benefit analysis, that appearance is misleading. Probability and cost estimates are essentially based on current understandings, and efficiency is a built-in value. By adopting this as a criterion embedded in a "value free" technique, other competing values can receive short shrift.

The decision-tree technique does differ from the cost-benefit approach in that the decision tree adapts more easily and usefully to decision situations where monetary units are not particularly important. For example, decision-tree analysis can be applied to military strategy or other situations where one has to assess the probability of an opponent's response. Natural disasters threatening human life or health are other situations where decisions could be informed by the nonmonetary probabilities associated with each choice alternative. Of course, even in this mode, decision-tree analysis continues to be limited by the exclusion of other possibilities once particular choices are articulated in the calculation and by the tenuous nature of estimated probabilities. William W. Lowrance suggests that these estimates may be closer to "votes" by the participants in the analysis than to reflections of the possibilities of actual occurrences.[33]

Simulations and Models

Simulations and models are techniques that represent attempts to create the equivalent of a laboratory setting to determine the likely outcomes of various policy choices. The result is a prediction in the following form: Given conditions X_1 through X_i, policy choices A_1 to A_i will have impacts Y_1 to Y_i. With this information, one would select the option that seems best—normally the most cost-effective option. The usual means of carrying this out is through computers and software packages. The goal of simulation and modeling techniques is to develop more rational control over decisions and to increase the odds that the actual policy adopted will be an efficient choice. These approaches tend to be fairly abstract in that through the construction of hypothetical relationships, they attempt to encompass a broad range of individual behavior.

Governments at the local level have increasingly purchased computer software models to try to rationalize the budget-making process. The computer models (in budgeting called Fiscal Impact Budgeting Systems, or FIBS) forecast government service needs and both expenditure and revenue needs over the next year to several years. The data base for projections includes previous expenditure and revenue levels, demographics, intergovernmental funding relationships, and predicted changes in each of these parameters. Kenneth L. Kraemer and William H. Dutton note that

> FIBS are a classic management-science response to a fundamental policy problem—that of developing more rational control by elected officials and the general public over decisions that affect the fiscal position of government. They are promoted as leading to improvements in information processing, content, and flows, and as such, they represent a potential tool for managerial rationalism.[34]

Generically, these FIBS produce predictions of the impact of different budgetary decisions. Such computer models also provide important tools for policy analysis in budget making at the national level, as both the Office of Management and Budget and the Congressional Budget Office employ complex simulations to discern potential impacts of different budgetary strategies.

Like cost-benefit analysis, modeling draws heavily on ideas from economics, especially in areas involving budgeting. Other models, of course, may *not* be based on economic assumptions. Examples would be those utilizing engineering principles or dealing with problems in air pollution. Many of the questions raised about this instrument of policy analysis are familiar. There is great uncertainty in decision situations, and computer simulations must necessarily oversimplify reality and be based on artificial assumptions. This is an outcome-oriented technique and, as a result, reflects utilitarian premises.

But in application, other problems occur as well. While the number of policy alternatives examined must be limited to be manageable, political bias often determines the boundaries of choice. Often, public officials specify that they want a choice between just A and B. This produces a prearranged, or "cooked," result if one of the options is obviously preferable to the other. The temptation exists for the political preferences of public officials to encourage manipulation of this "scientific" technique. And, as the reader shall see in chapters 4 and 5, political pressures on elected officials produce short-term thinking that can overwhelm the results of policy analysis—or lead to skewing of analyses for political ends. With or without overt political concerns, the analyst must make initial choices in modeling. The essential point is that he or she should remain aware of the ramifications of these choices for later policy decisions.

In fact, their amenability to manipulation through control of the choice of alternatives to be considered renders all three of the techniques discussed especially vulnerable in the policy process. Students of policy analysis, such as Stokey and Zeckhauser, are fully aware of the possibilities in this respect and caution that the legitimacy of policy analysis depends on everyone playing by the rules. Speaking directly to this issue with regard to cost-benefit analysis, they note that outright deception can involve "submerged assumptions, unfairly chosen valuations, and purposeful misestimates," and add the caveat that "any procedure for making policy choices, from divine guidance to computer algorithms, can be manipulated unfairly."[35] Certainly, the last statement has merit, but the essential point that should not escape the policy analyst is that the aura of objectivity conveyed by the techniques used has a tendency to clothe them with some of the immutability once reserved for divine guidance. Yet as James M. Buchanan and Marilyn R. Flowers point out, these techniques applied by the most fair-minded and circumspect of analytical technicians will involve opportunity costs. They will deemphasize or omit certain possibilities or opportunities in their formulation.[36] Once these techniques are subjected to the powerful hydraulic forces of the political system, there are few guarantees that they will be able to withstand skewing and twisting for partisan purposes, although the use of technical communities specially designed for quality control and review may provide some barrier to such skewing. Agencies under pressure to undertake projects may find themselves sorely tempted to underestimate their costs and ignore viable alternatives in their efforts to win legislative approval.

Experimental Analysis

The final tool examined here is social experimentation. Using this approach, the analyst would examine results from quasi experiments or—ideally— true experiments to determine the best course of action. The true social experiment relies on random assignment of subjects to an experimental group receiving the services of the program being tested and a control group not receiving those services. Experiments are normally conducted with pilot or demonstration studies to see if the experimental programs should become general policy. If those assigned to the experimental group benefit more than those in control groups, that is considered evidence that the program has had a positive benefit (i.e., it "works"). In contrast, the quasi experiment proceeds without random assignment of subjects and is therefore less rigorous procedurally. This approach, while often the best available given the constraints of particular situations, usually cannot produce results with the same level of validity as those from the more rigorous experimental design. It attempts to apply the scientific method of the natural sciences through the social sciences (especially sociology and political science).

An impressive array of policy experiments has been carried out from the late 1960s through the present. Among them are various income main- tenance (negative income tax or guaranteed annual income) experiments, housing allowance programs, Aid to Families with Dependent Children (AFDC) adjustments, and voucher-type plans for educational expenses. Os- tensibly, the goal has been to use results from these pilot studies to help design better programs on a large scale. In these instances, the policy analyst can base policy recommendations on actual experiments, carried out in a "real world" setting.

In one negative income tax (NIT) experiment, almost 1400 low-in- come, male-headed families in metropolitan areas in New Jersey and Penn- sylvania took part. Participants were randomly assigned to one of eight ex- perimental groups or to the control group. Each experimental cohort was governed by a different negative income tax structure (different levels of guaranteed income and different tax rates). Every two weeks, a check was sent to experimental subjects. The amount of the checks was computed by a formula based on the family's income and the structure of the specific experimental NIT. Families were interviewed every three months over a three-year period to try to determine if a guaranteed income would create a work disincentive and how much such a program would cost if imple- mented on a larger scale.

The NIT experiment indicates why the impact of social experimentation has been minimal. Full experiments take much time to complete. Often, by the time results are made available, the program has become a "dead issue" for one reason or another. The policy cycle begins with public interest aroused about a specific problem. Experiments may then be undertaken by government. But by the time results are in, the citizenry's interest has waned, and impetus for change has dissipated. When final results of the income maintenance experiments came in under the Nixon administration, political conditions were no longer ripe for enactment of such a policy. Furthermore, after the experiment was well under way, officials became interested in a "work for welfare" component; however, it was by then too late to include this critical element in the experiments. Not surprisingly, opponents of programs have seen the use of the experimental technique as a way of delaying action on a major commitment until it can be safely killed.[37]

Basic technical problems abound with conducting experiments in a social setting. They include the sometimes difficult task of just getting enough participants, the resistance of prospective subjects to "being experimented on," the tendency of experimental programs to "drift" (i.e., to evolve over time) and render uncertain how the program actually affected people, and the question of external validity (How generalizable to other settings are the results of a particular social experiment?).

In addition to technical problems with constructing a valid experimental design, there are serious normative limitations on how it can be used. For instance, to construct a "tight" experimental design, can one withhold services from some while supplying them to others? Ethical considerations prevent a wide variety of experiments on humans. When ethics are ignored, as in the Tuskegee quasi experiments of the 1930s, in which a group of over 400 blacks was not treated for syphilis in order to study the disease's progress over decades, the results are grotesque and a violation of the subjects' basic rights.[38]

Ethical and technical problems do not exhaust the difficulties associated with social experimentation and its ability to provide firm data for the policy analyst. In the larger projects, a tremendous amount of interpretation and subjective selection is inherent in the experimental process. The initial steps of defining a social problem to be examined must reflect someone's normative perspective. The selection of kinds of intervention again raises the problem of opportunity costs in that this decision will eliminate further consideration of other forms of intervention, some of which might seem equally urgent from other value perspectives. Finally, interpretation of the results of a social experiment admit of a wide variety of views, and individuals from different normative perspectives may agree on the substance of the findings but differ heatedly on whether the proposed social intervention was a success or a failure. The NIT experiments are but one example of this phenomenon.

The difficulties in the adequate performance of policy analysis are thus numerous. But the intention of this section has not been to discredit the technical procedures described, only to warn against naive belief in the power of analytical objectivity. For example, despite their problems, the NIT experiments have been used in debates over welfare reform. With all their faults, the alternative to using the techniques described is to rely on hunch and guesswork—hardly methods to be recommended.

The Policy Process

At its most basic level, policy analysis operates under the assumption that decision making ought to be a more rational process; analytic methods are assumed to enhance rationality in the policy process. Rationality does not describe very well how decisions are actually made, however. The very way in which humans think can lead to their values being more important in decision-making situations than purely rational conclusions based on policy analysis. To understand policy making, one must understand policy-makers' values. Analysts may underestimate the significance of decision-makers' values and overestimate the persuasive value of policy analysis. In addition, political considerations can elevate voters' values over policy analysis.[39] Elected public officials must receive public support for reelection; consequently, mass values, even if not always sensible or coherent, can override policy analysis.

Knowledge of the policy process—and the role of values in it—is important for the policy analyst. James Anderson summarizes the overall implications.

The policy-making process in the United States is an adversarial process, characterized by the clash of competing and conflicting viewpoints and interests rather than an impartial, disinterested, or "objective" search for "correct" solutions for policy problems. Public officials—

legislators, administrators, and perhaps to a lesser extent, judges —do not stand impartially about [*sic*] the policy struggle. Rather, they have their own values and positions which they seek to advance and hence are often partisans in the policy struggle. Given this, policy analyses done by social scientists, for instance, may have little impact except as they provide support for the positions of particular participants in the policy process.[40]

The whole policy process is messy, replete with considerable randomness, but careful research can have an important impact—from agenda setting through the implementation stage. The policy analyst is in a position to add an element of rationality to this process and to increase the likelihood of programs operating successfully. Although this impact may not be exactly what analysts have hoped for, it adds an important degree of enlightenment to the policy process that might not otherwise have been there.

To be understood properly, policy analysis must be examined within the context of the larger policy process. Normally, the policy process is seen as a series of stages. Three of these steps—agenda setting, decision making, and implementation—are sufficiently critical to the policy analyst to warrant examination here. Agenda setting occurs when decision makers conclude that an issue must be considered in the policy process. Some problems are seen as worthy of debate; others are not. Decision making describes the process of formulating policies in response to issues that are on the agenda. Finally, these policies must be implemented, or actually put into effect.

The analyst must understand that the different values and perspectives brought to bear at each phase of the policy process can determine the definition of the issue at that point. Policy actors at each stage redefine the issue in terms relevant to their particular context. This can begin as early as the agenda-setting stage. For example, the Equal Rights Amendment may have been seen by many as a means for creating greater legal protection for women, but for others it was important to have it on the agenda as a rallying point for keeping the feminist movement vibrant.

As issues move into the legislative branch, a wide variety of concerns, at times with little relevance to the issue as the analyst once described it, come to bear. An instance of the intrusion of extraneous concerns into consideration of a policy issue occurred in the 1960s when, in an effort to aid the less developed countries, some senators supported the export of powdered fish to these nations. Unfortunately, they labeled the substance *fish flour,* thereby drawing the immediate and intense opposition of America's wheat farmers. These farmers might have opposed the export in any event, but use of the term "flour" served to intensify their opposition by making it appear that powdered fish was in direct competition with their product. Other examples of diversion from the original issue are frequent at this stage of policy making.

The administrative and judicial sectors are not exceptions to the principle that issues become hostages to the various contexts of the policy process. Administrators have their own interests to promote. In fact, William Niskanen has advanced a theory of bureaucracy that assumes that administrators are primarily interested in increased salaries and more prestige, power, and patronage.[41] Courts also have perspectives ingrained in their approaches to issues that have a redefinitional effect. The power of judicial precedent and the configurations of an issue provided by opposing attorneys can greatly influence a court's views, as well as reshape the definition of the issue.

The politically astute analyst, then, will understand that his or her data and the recommendations carefully based on those data can easily become sidetracked by other considerations as the issue moves through the policy process. The label on the issue may remain the same, but the contents undergo continual change. As a consequence, policy makers who appear to be debating an issue as originally defined are actually often contesting other questions of more importance and personal interest to them.

Agenda Setting

The agenda reflects the basic power patterns of the policy process and is the crucial first step for any proposal. If no one wishes to discuss a proposal, obviously its supporters are nonplayers and it is a nonissue in the policy process. While the process by which problems are placed on the agenda is tangled, there are nonetheless regularities. Three basic elements help to shape what gets on the governmental agenda: problems, politics, and visible participants.[42]

First, if some condition is not identified as a problem, it will not be placed on the agenda. Statistical indicators (e.g., the number of people living in poverty) may show that a condition is growing into a real problem. This may force government officials to place more emphasis on this issue. Events such as natural disasters can focus attention on a particular condition and increase the odds that it will be put on the agenda. Getting officials to believe that there is a problem is a key first step in agenda setting, and at this point analysts, within and outside government, can have significant influence by providing data and framing the dimensions of the problem.

A second set of factors that affect agenda setting is political. A kind of consensus may emerge that certain circumstances call for government consideration; this consensus is often a product of bargaining, negotiation, and compromise among the multitude of actors.

Third, visible political actors are central in deciding what to decide about. Among them are the President, Congress, key high-level appointees, top administrators, media, parties, and interest groups. If few or none of the visible actors is in favor of placing a problem on the agenda, it is highly unlikely that it will be considered.

Values are key factors at this stage. For instance, one value having some impact is equity, the redress of imbalances or unfairness. Proposals can get onto the agenda if an existing policy is seen as unfair, even if proposed remedies are more inefficient. Equity as a value may override policy analysis based on efficiency criteria. The implementation of affirmative action plans, for example, may require adjustments in the interests of long-term fairness that cause considerable dislocation and inconvenience in the short term.

The policy analyst does have a role in the agenda-setting process by helping to identify conditions that may come to be seen as problems and, hence, deserving of agenda placement, even if he or she does not have great overt impact on getting an issue put on the agenda. The analyst can also help develop the alternative proposals that "bubble up" through various policy communities and become adopted by visible political actors. Finally, analysts can help to frame discussion of an issue in a specialized language that places policy competitors at a disadvantage. Thus, by structuring issues in terms of systems analysis, Secretary of Defense McNamara's "whiz kids" were able to gain increased leverage over the Joint Chiefs of Staff, who were less conversant in the argot of policy analysis.

Decision Making

When or whether policy alternatives get taken up seriously is partially a chance proposition. The process depends to some extent on unpredictable events, on political currents, and on the desires of visible political actors. Policy analysts play important, although less visible, roles in beginning to develop alternatives that can then be considered once some condition is defined as a problem to be placed on the political agenda. These alternatives form a "policy stream" that flows parallel to the current of events. At some point, appropriate policy proposals that have been under tentative consideration may be coupled with the pressure to "do something" about a problem that events have propelled onto the agenda.

Formulation of policies or specification of policy alternatives is only one part of the actual decision-making portion of the policy process. Officials must then select one policy from the number of policies described by John Kingdon as "floating around."[43] Decision making, ultimately, means adopting a particular policy and providing at least some budgetary support for it. At the national level, key actors include the President, his advisers and top administrative appointees, Congress, interest groups, and interested agencies. To get approval of a policy, *normally*, majority coalitions must be developed. This means that a process of negotiation and compromise among many of the parties with a stake in the policy takes place.

The role of public opinion or the national mood is taken into account by decision makers. One common result is incremental decision making, with the new policy tending to be a tinkering with existing policies or a series of changes on the margins of the status quo. A final characteristic of the process as a result of these different considerations is a short-term perspective on decisions that coincides with the two-year election cycles of Congress.

Findings from psychology suggest that, in general, people who make decisions under conditions of uncertainty—quite common in the political world—use certain "rules of thumb," or "heuristics."[44] That is, when facts are not clear and when the context in which decisions are made is murky, people adopt nonrational shortcuts in order to facilitate making decisions. One frequent characteristic of decision making in such circumstances is the central importance of an individual policy-maker's preexisting values and beliefs. People interpret uncertain facts to comport with their values and beliefs; their preconceptions shape the types of information used in decision making. One common consequence is inappropriate use of historical events. Time and again, policy makers have succumbed to the temptation to interpret a current problem in terms of a controversy from their past when more objective examination would have uncovered important differences.

Values and decision-making shortcuts used by policy makers play a large role in determining which choices leaders will actually make under the common conditions of uncertainty. The use of personal values and beliefs for heuristic shortcuts to decisions has been especially noticeable in foreign policy. Foreign policy decision makers often develop "value screens" that influence their decisions. These images act as powerful filters and affect their perceptions and expectations. During the Eisenhower administration, Secretary of State John Foster Dulles seemed to ignore important information before the Suez Crisis in 1956. An operational code study indicates that Dulles's belief system led him to interpret Soviet behavior as "bad" and British behavior as "good"—ignoring, as a result, obvious signs that Britain planned to join with France and Israel to attack Egypt. Apparently Dulles's belief that Britain would do nothing to harm American policy interests (one attribute of a "good" state) acted to screen out clear nonconfirming evidence.[45]

On the domestic front, personal value priorities must also be taken into account. Surely, President Ronald Reagan's threefold tax and budget strategy elaborated on during his 1980 presidential campaign (tax cuts plus increased defense spending plus a balanced budget) was constructed on his deeply held beliefs about the role of government and the primacy of a strong defense. The value screen was so strong that Reagan did not seem to hear David Stockman's continual warnings about a massive federal deficit and the likely ensuing economic difficulties. Similarly, when Howard Baker, known as a person adept at negotiation and compromise, became President Reagan's chief of staff, he soon learned that some of the President's positions were simply not open to discussion.

Whether or not historical scripts are employed seems to depend on how easily they are recalled by decision makers and the links with their basic values. Historical events that are most vivid and intimately tied to personal values and experiences tend to be selected for application in decision making. Jimmy Carter's overloading of Congress with a blizzard of policy initiatives during the first few months of his Presidency may be partially explained through his use of the "100 Days" historical script. He was captivated by the success achieved during the first hundred days of Franklin Roosevelt's administration (and, to a lesser extent, that of Lyndon Johnson). He was convinced that, based on the analogy with FDR and LBJ, if he wished to have a real impact as President, he had to act quickly, during the purported "honeymoon" period with Congress. Unhappily, although the "100 Days" script was vivid in Carter's mind, it was not applicable to his situation. The nation was neither in the midst of a depression nor mourning the loss of a recently assassinated President. Congress became overloaded, and the bulk of his initiatives came to naught.[46]

In short, policy analysis is not likely to provide the clear, unassailable data needed to cause decision makers to abandon or change their preexisting values and beliefs in policy situations. The values of decision makers must be taken into account by policy analysts because they are important in shaping the decisions made by political officials.

Implementation
The central figures in the often invisible implementation stage of the policy process are administrators in the agencies charged with putting a paper policy into operation. But high-level officials in the executive branch or legislators can have an effect by serving as "fixers," prodding, if necessary, the bureaucracies in charge of implementation. Other actors can get involved too. Interest groups with a stake in the specific program may have real influence; judges (through judicial review of agency regulations) can be key players.

The major contribution of policy analysts to implementation would appear to occur at the policy formulation stage. Here policy analysts can have an impact on program administration by having the foresight to build into their analyses specifications that increase the odds of successful implementation later. They can also have considerable influence through their evaluation of the effectiveness of a program, especially if they conclude that implementation procedures are hampering a program.

Personal values play an important role in aiding or hindering implementation. Because administrators often have considerable discretion in how they implement policy, their attitudes toward a program are important. If their values differ from those of the decision makers who formulated the policy, they are in a position to shape the program to fit more closely their own views. As an example, the opposition of the Office of Education to the goals of Title I of the 1965 Education Act and to the National Teacher Corps contained in the same act reshaped both programs dramatically after they were enacted into law.[47] This potential for slippage between decision and implementation is a particularly important consideration for the analyst formulating approaches toward dealing with a problem.

Policy Analysis and the Policy Process
Policy analysts have accumulated and developed numerous techniques that are sophisticated and powerful in their capacity for providing data, analyzing relationships, and clarifying alternatives. Yet the use of analysts' work

in the policy process remains limited, a problem that can be traced to its vulnerability to other forces.

First, decision makers often are faced with information overload. Especially when highly controversial issues are being considered, congressmen, administrators, and even judges can be deluged with studies and recommendations from many contending sources. The result can easily be that all information becomes diluted in persuasiveness, and the decision maker feels more comfortable relying on less rationally defensible but more personally satisfying modes of reaching a solution.

Second, the use of analysis primarily for reinforcement of already made choices seems to be a common feature of political reality. Patton found that political considerations affected use of evaluation research in fifteen of the twenty cases he studied.[48] David Whiteman, in his study of Congress's OTA, found that political-strategic use of analytical findings was greatest in the most controversial, conflictual, and visible cases. These post hoc uses may serve to protect individual members of Congress from electoral retribution.[49]

A third problem is the politicization of research. An agency's analyses may be countered by studies carried out by opposing researchers hired by interest groups and other political actors. This can lead people to see research as a commodity to be bought and sold, and devoid of any intrinsic value. Cynicism about the usefulness of "scientific" findings can easily result. If some research suggests that acid rain comes from midwestern manufacturing plants and is devastating eastern forests and lakes, one can easily predict that there will emerge countervailing analyses from representatives of the accused economic interests.

A fourth problem is overtly political: Policy analysts often lack an independent power base or political acumen. Many times, to have influence, the analyst has to link up with a client who possesses power. Meltsner asserts that the agency policy analyst "does not have a constituency to support him when he is in trouble; and like the staff person who relies on the holder of a position, the analyst is dependent on his client."[50] Sometimes, analysts may be politically innocent, not understanding the importance of political considerations. Part of this may result from the economics background common to many analysts. This can facilitate narrow, technically proficient analysis of a problem without adequate regard for the administrative or political process, an approach characteristic of the analyst operating in the technician role described earlier. Elected officials must take into account many other factors, however—such as the attractiveness of the policy to voters and the implications of a decision for personal career goals—in addition to technical validity and efficiency. Another value taken seriously by policy makers, and less seriously by some analysts, is equity, since the public finds fairness an important criterion for policy.

Fifth, policy analysts may provide useful information about a particular policy, yet give very little guidance on how the policy should be implemented. Robert A. Scott and Arnold R. Shore, for example, note that, because they fail to understand the constraints on policy makers, "sociologists sometimes produce recommendations that are implausible, impractical and unrealistic."[51] Meltsner says that analysts should move beyond defining policy to consideration of how it can be put into effect.[52] Policy analysts ought to put a higher priority on implementation issues, such as how the program can best be put into operation and administered, than they currently do. More concrete consideration of the "how to do it" issues would increase the instrumental use of policy analysis. This suggests, more generally, the importance to policy analysts of linking their analysis more closely to the broader policy process within which it is embedded. Given the indirect "enlightenment" impact of policy analysis, this becomes an important tactical consideration.

One final factor that cannot be overemphasized is the importance of the values of the participants—from policy analysts to policy makers to the general public—in the policy process. For the policy analyst to maximize his or her role as adviser, this basic but often ignored reality must be fully appreciated. Rational-scientific analysis can assist in approaching social life, but it can neither supplant nor entirely explain its normative core.

Notes

1. Bryan Magee, *Men of Ideas* (New York: Oxford University Press, 1982), 107.

2. Karl Popper, *Unended Quest* (La Salle, Ill.: Open Court, 1976), 141–51.

3. John Dewey, *Liberalism and Social Action* (New York: Capricorn Books, 1935), 27.

4. John Dewey, *The Public and Its Problems* (Chicago: Gateway Press, 1946), 208–9.

5. Harold D. Lasswell, *A Pre-View of Policy Sciences* (New York: American Elsevier, 1971), xiii–xiv.

6. Laurence H. Tribe, "Policy Science : Analysis or Ideology?" *Philosophy and Public Affairs* 2 (Fall 1972): 85.

7. Jeremy Bentham, *An Introduction to the Principles of Morals and Legislation* (New York: Hafner Publishing, 1948 [1789]), 2.

8. Charles Murray, *Losing Ground: American Social Policy, 1950–1980* (New York: Basic Books, 1984).

9. Anthony Downs, *Inside Bureaucracy* (Boston: Little, Brown, 1967).

10. Arnold D. Meltsner, *Policy Analysts in the Bureaucracy* (Berkeley: University of California Press, 1976), 168.

11. Lawrence M. Mead, "Science versus Analysis: A False Dichotomy," *Journal of Policy Analysis and Management* 4 (Spring 1985): 421.

12. Charles W. Anderson, "The Place of Principles in Policy Analysis," *American Political Science Review* 73 (September 1979): 717.

13. Ibid.

14. Ibid., 719.

15. Grover Starling, *The Politics and Economics of Public Policy* (Homewood, Ill.: Dorsey Press, 1979).

16. Michael Quinn Patton, *Utilization-Focused Evaluation* (Beverley Hills: Sage, 1978), 34.

17. David Whiteman, "The Fate of Policy Analysis in Congressional Decision-Making," *Western Political Quarterly* 38 (June 1985): 294–311.

18. Peter W. House and Roger D. Shull, *Rush to Policy* (New Brunswick, N.J.: Transaction, 1988), 181.

19. Robert F. Rich, "Uses of Social Science Information by Federal Bureaucracies" in *Using Social Research in Public Policy Making,* ed. Carol H. Weiss (Lexington, Mass.: Lexington Press, 1977), 199–212.

20. Carol H. Weiss, "Policy Research in the Context of Diffuse Decision-Making " in *Social Science Research and Public Policy-Making,* ed. D.B.P. Kallen et al. (Windsor, England: NFER-Nelson, 1982), 534.

21. Carol H. Weiss and Michael J. Bucuvalas, "Truth Tests and Utility Tests," *American Sociological Review* 45 (April 1980): 302–13.

22. Meltsner, *Policy Analysts,* 14–15.

23. Emil J. Posavac and Raymond G. Carey, *Program Evaluation* (Englewood Cliffs, N.J.: Prentice-Hall, 1985), 263–64.

24. House and Shull comment on these difficulties from the view of practicing policy analysts in *Rush to Policy,* 21–48.

25. See John D. Graham and James W. Vaupel, "The Value of a Life," in *What Role for Government?* ed. Richard J. Zeckhauser and Derek Leebaert (Durham, N.C.: Duke University Press, 1983), 176–86.

26. Aaron Wildavsky, "The Political Economy of Efficiency," *Public Administration Review* 4 (December 1966): 296.

27. Edith Stokey and Richard Zeckhauser, *A Primer for Policy Analysis* (New York: Norton, 1978), 286.

28. Edmund Burke, *Reflections on the Revolution in France,* ed. Thomas H.D. Mahoney (Indianapolis: Bobbs-Merrill, 1955 [1790]), 110.

29. Tribe, "Policy Science," 82.

30. Stokey and Zeckhauser, *A Primer,* 201.

31. Susan Welch and John C. Comer, *Quantitative Methods for Public Administration* (Homewood, Ill.: Dorsey Press, 1983), 266.

32. William W. Lowrance, *Modern Science and Human Values* (New York: Oxford University Press, 1985), 142–49.

33. Ibid., 122.

34. Kenneth L. Kraemer and William H. Dutton, "The Automation of Bias" in *Computers and Politics,* ed. James N. Danziger et al. (New York: Columbia University Press, 1982), 190.

35. Stokey and Zeckhauser, *A Primer,* 135.

36. James M. Buchanan and Marilyn R. Flowers, *The Public Finances,* 4th ed. (Homewood, Ill.: Irwin, 1975), 183–84.

37. David H. Greenberg and Philip K. Robins, "The Changing Role of Social Experiments in Policy Analysis," *Journal of Policy Analysis and Management* 5 (Winter 1986): 340–62.

38. Jean Heller, "Syphilis Victims in U.S. Study Went Untreated for Forty Years," *New York Times,* 26 July 1972, 1, 8.

39. House and Shull, *Rush to Policy,* 175–81.

40. James E. Anderson, *Public Policy-Making,* 3d ed. (New York: Holt, Rinehart and Winston, 1984), 163.

41. William Niskanen, *Bureaucracy and Representative Government* (Chicago: Aldine-Atherton, 1971).

42. See especially John W. Kingdon, *Agendas, Alternatives, and Public Policy* (Boston: Little, Brown, 1984).

43. Ibid.

44. For example, Daniel Kahneman, Paul Slovic, and Amos Tversky, ed., *Judgment under Uncertainty* (Cambridge: Cambridge University Press, 1982).

45. Stephen G. Walker and Timothy G. Murphy, "The Utility of the Operational Code in Political Forecasting," *Political Psychology* 3 (Spring-Summer 1981–82): 24–60.

46. Richard Neustadt and Ernest R. May, *Thinking in Time* (New York: Free Press, 1986), 66–74.

47. Thomas E. Cronin, "Small Programs, Big Troubles: Policy Making for a Small Great Society Program" in *American Politics and Public Policy*, ed. Walter Dean Burnham and Martha Wagner Weinberg (Cambridge, Mass.: MIT Press, 1978), 77–108.

48. Patton, *Utilization-Focused Evaluation*.

49. Whiteman, "The Fate of Policy Analysis."

50. Meltsner, *Policy Analysts*, 157.

51. Robert A. Scott and Arnold R. Shore, *Why Sociology Does Not Apply* (New York: Elsevier, 1979), 29.

52. Meltsner, *Policy Analysts*, 269.

CHAPTER 3

The Cultural Setting of Policy Analysis

The last two chapters have examined the values implicit in the concept of policy analysis, in roles the analyst plays and in techniques the analyst employs in his or her work. Also mentioned was the importance of the values the analyst brings to the workplace, as a citizen and as a person. These are mirrored in or contradicted by the values of clients. And they are embodied in or opposed to ways in which the policy issues are defined for the analyst. They also find their way into the studies an analyst produces.

An examination of those values indicates that they reflect the complexity of American society and its past. They are a paradoxical structure of notions put together under the name "American political culture." Sometimes they appear to be a mere potpourri, but there is an underlying order to them, the structure of which can be delineated.[1] This takes the form of a patterned political culture and systematic ethical systems that mirror that culture.

Gilbert and Sullivan sang that "everyone who's born into this world a-*live* is either a little *lib*-er-al, or else a Con-ser-va-*tive*." Today, the choices in America are more varied: old-fashioned welfare liberal, cultural conservative, economic conservative, Yuppie libertarian, neoconservative, left-leaning liberal, communitarian, various Marxist tendencies, and more. One of the more remarkable things about this motley array of ideological positions is that they all tend to contain more or less the same vocabulary, though the words are differently nuanced and positioned in the various theories, weighted differently, and differently combined. Also, when one moves away from that small group of intellectuals whose chief employment is to define and defend ideological positions and from political and economic leadership circles into the general public, it becomes difficult to discover groups of people who subscribe to thought-out, coherent ideological positions, as well as ideological groups that are stable over time.

Whatever combination of values an analyst brings to his or her desk, it will be, in part, a mixture attributable to a number of environmental

68

influences. They include having been born in a family with a particular tradition, having a particular social status, hailing from a particular region of the country, having been raised during a particular period of time, being employed by a particular agency. But the analyst's value ideas will also have uniqueness; they will be the values of a particular person who has had unique experiences. In this chapter it is necessary to concentrate on central themes and concepts that constitute the general—on the cultural materials out of which individuals in America fashion their world views and arrive at their ethical judgments.

Liberty and Equality: The Politics of Conscience and the Politics of Interest

Two concepts form the core of American political culture: the ideas of liberty and equality. Each has been variously defined over the years, sometimes in ways that support one another, other times in antagonistic fashion. Both have been focused on the individual and have been expressed in terms of individual rights. Each has also played a role in two sets of ideas and attitudes that have dominated American thought over the years: a politics of conscience and a politics of interest.

The politics of conscience manifested itself for the first time in American life in the Puritan "New Jerusalem" of colonial Massachusetts, a "city built upon a hill." In this society, whose structure mirrored in salient ways the theocentric organicism of premodern Europe, the good of the individual was realized in fulfilling God's law, which was identified with the common good. Service of this objective good was also declared the substance of civil liberty. This was a liberty "to that only which is good, just, and honest ... exercised in a subjection to authority."[2] With this view of liberty was paired a concept of the equal worth of all men and women in the eyes of God. Ralph Barton Perry has called this "generic equality" and explained it as

> the idea that beneath the clothes they wear, and the status or occupation which organized society has bestowed upon them, all men are men, with the same faculties, the same needs and aspirations, the same destiny, and similar potentialities of development.... No one will deny it, once the question is raised in this form.[3]

The politics of conscience in Puritan times also displayed a concept of individual liberty rather different from the one just characterized, a concept that has frequently come into conflict with the notion that liberty must be defined in relation to a publicly sanctioned standard of morality. It was represented in the antinomian stance of Anne Hutchinson, who asserted that God's will can be revealed directly to the individual, apart from authoritative interpretations of Scripture by church ministers supported by public authority. Her insistence on personal autonomy eventuated in Anne Hutchinson's persecution by the leaders of the Bay Colony and eventually in her banishment. The pluralist society of today has worked out the antinomian conception of freedom in great secular detail and embodied it in laws that give wide protection to individual freedom of choice in life style. It is also represented in the concept of patient autonomy in the face of the paternal authority of the physician, as well as in disputes about a woman's right to control her body.

The politics of interest has also been part of American political culture from the earliest days. But in this frame of reference, liberty and equality receive a very different definition and are differently related to one another. In the politics of interest, liberty is understood as security and as the right to accumulate private property. It is a politics of material well-being. Its terms of reference were fashioned in the seventeenth century out of the rising commercial culture of that time and eminently given voice by James Harrington, a classical republican political theorist schooled in the egoistic political philosophy of Niccolo Machiavelli.[4] But it was not Machiavelli of *The Prince* but the republican enthusiast of *The Discourses* upon whom Harrington drew for inspiration. Politics in this framework is conceived as a realm of strategic maneuver and rational calculation among self-interested individuals who wish to win in the great game of life. As a republican theory, it envisages the competition of individuals taking place within a system of rules that break up concentrations of power and limit its exercise through institutional balance.

Harrington saw economic self-interest rather than generalized selfishness as the dominant human motive. C.B. Macpherson has pointed up evidence of his "awareness of and acceptance of market motivations and relationships."[5] Harrington also joined freedom to acquire with the work ethic, which Puritanism had bred deeply into American life, in observing that property is gained by industry, not by mere ambition. He also recognized that commercial and urban society was tremendously productive, and that it is the "natural operation of a law of supply and demand ... that brings the secondary growth."[6] Harrington's philosophy expressed well the optimistic individualism of the middle-class settlers of seventeenth-century

America. And his constitutional prescriptions for the defense of liberty are found written large on many colonial charters.

Conscience and Interest in Ethical Theory

In the last ten years there has been a proliferation of courses in ethics in developing public policy programs. This has resulted in part from an awareness that traditional standards do not furnish ethical models for a score of new ethical problems that have been spawned by the growth of technology. It is also a fruit of change in American political culture, and in particular of changes in the balance between authoritative norms of moral respectability and a rapid increase in claims of individual liberty. Ethicists have responded by adapting their formal ethical systems to the analysis of public policy dilemmas that confront analysts and decision makers.

Since ethicists have been bred in the same moral culture as other Americans, it is not surprising that the systems they employ bear a remarkable resemblance to the politics of conscience and the politics of interest that are under discussion. Deontological or Kantian ethics places special value on the rights and dignity of every person because of the individual's freedom and rationality. This school of thought grounds the special worth of the individual on his or her ability to understand principles of right and freely to respond to them rather than to the dictates of desire. Utilitarianism, by contrast, is concerned with the social good, quantitatively considered. Its fundamental rule is that public policy should aim at maximizing the utilities of society as a whole. Most utilitarians assume, like the adherents of the politics of interest, that the sole legitimate basis of social good is what individuals happen to value. And they view the process of social choice as an aggregative one, in which individual preferences are added to one another in arriving at decisions on the substance of social welfare. Utilitarians, however, have no principle for distributing social values. Their criterion of judgment is the criterion of maximum social product—efficiency.

The Politics of Conscience Today

The understanding of liberty as grounded in obedience to moral law and of equality as referring to fundamental worth are still powerful notions in American life. The importance of morality, especially in the models of character that leaders present to the general public for their emulation, has been highlighted in the reaction to recent scandals involving public figures. In a 1987 national telephone survey, 74 percent of the sample lamented the failure of leaders to set good examples. "Ethics, often dismissed as a prissy Sunday School word, is now at the center of a new national debate.... Has the mindless materialism of the '80s left in its wake a values vacuum?" asks a writer for *Time* magazine.[7] Another writer in the same issue observes that the "good idea" on which America was founded "combines a commitment to man's inalienable rights with the Calvinist belief in an ultimate moral right and sinful man's obligation to do good."[8]

A good deal of work has recently been done on the idea of equality as a salient concept of American political culture. One particularly significant study was carried out by Jennifer Hochschild, a professor of political science, who conducted open-ended interviews with twenty-eight working adults in New Haven, Connecticut. The respondents were chosen at random from the lowest-income and highest-income neighborhoods of the city. The book that resulted from this experience is a splendid qualitative description of attitudes toward equality defined in a variety of ways. Remark ably, Hochschild found an extraordinary agreement across social and economic lines, both in affirmation and rejection of the value of equality. She also found ambivalence toward equality, as well as tensions and psychological conflicts, that cut across social groups. The book is in part an update and extension of Robert Lane's pioneering study of 1962, *Political Ideology: Why the American Common Man Believes What He Does.*[9]

The Right to Equal Opportunity

Hochschild found that rich and poor alike strongly support the principle of equality in "the socializing domain—the arena of home, family, school, and neighborhood" (p. 44). In epitomizing the beliefs of one respondent, she remarks that "the fact of equal human worth and the obligation it imposes on socializing agencies to seek equal well-being for all—these principles matter more than any specific normative claim" (p. 106). Here is a value that is squarely in the tradition of the politics of conscience. One of Hochschild's poor respondents told her that schoolteachers "*should* help the ones that can't do it, the less smart ones. They need it. I believe in that." She also thought that teachers ought not to compare their students with one another to their faces, as this would make the less able feel bad (p. 86). Compassion requires that all be treated as equal. For though people may not be of equal skill, they ought still be accorded equal respect (p. 88). Another needy respondent thought competition in the classroom, as in the economic domain, of great importance as a stimulant to incentive. But he defined the teacher's role in an egalitarian fashion: disproportionate help should be given to the one who needs it most (p. 94). One of Hochschild's well-to-do respondents remembered skipping collections from poor customers of her parents' fuel company in the 1930s depression. People have an obligation to respond to others' needs, without expecting gratitude (p. 102). Another found no place for even structured competition in the classroom. Instead, schools ought to be flexible enough to move gifted students along and to help the poor ones as well (p. 105). The same respondent thought a community is obliged to equalize its members' chances to succeed and be happy; the needy ought to be subsidized to be sure "everybody [has] a fair shot at a happy life." The talented can take care of themselves (p. 105). All this seems to fit under the heading of a broadly agreed social obligation to ensure equality of opportunity.

The Findings of Survey Research

Survey research statistically bears out the results of Hochschild's qualitative study in a single urban area. In a survey done between 1975 and 1977, respondents overwhelmingly embraced the egalitarian response, despite efforts to word the items to make inegalitarian replies acceptable. Asked to choose among three different ways of completing a sentence that began: "Teaching that some kinds of people are better than others"—74 percent both of the general public and of opinion leaders chose the alternative that ran: "goes against the American idea of equality." Only 12 percent of the public (and 8 percent of opinion leaders) chose the phrase: "only recognizes the facts." In the same survey, the corollary notion that society should give people, who are all of equal worth, an equal opportunity to succeed was embraced even more enthusiastically—by 78 percent of the general public and 82 percent of opinion leaders. ("Most of the people who are poor and needy could contribute something valuable to society if given the chance."[10]) Like Hochschild's respondents, the general public also places special emphasis on equality of educational opportunity.[11]

These findings coexist with the fact that American life has displayed rampant racial, ethnic, and religious prejudices and discrimination over the generations. Historical injustices to blacks and Native Americans are also blatant facts of American history, along with ill treatment of newly arrived immigrants of minority ethnic origin. Ethnocentrism has been an American tradition that contradicts the cultural egalitarianism. But it appears that the civil rights movement of the 1960s and 1970s has severely eroded such prejudice. Political leaders now avoid making statements that suggest racial prejudice. And in a 1978 survey, only 15 percent of white respondents expressed the belief that blacks are inferior to whites. In another recent survey, only 30 percent of the public were ready to agree that "like fine race horses, some classes of people are just naturally better than others," in contrast with almost 50 percent in the 1950s. Most Americans, however, acknowledge that *individuals* may differ in talent and capacity.[12]

Political Equality and Community: The Idea of "The People"
Although limited to property holders in the eighteenth century, the franchise became a prerogative of all white males by the Jacksonian period. It included both equal electoral right and an equal right to hold office. The process of constitutional amendment has since served to broaden the franchise to include first blacks and, much later, women. In the James Prothro and Charles Grigg study of American values carried out in the late 1950s, 95 percent of the sample affirmed that "every citizen should have an equal chance to influence government policy." [13] As data of 1958 and of 1978–79 show, a substantial majority of the general public and an even larger majority of influentials also favor equal voting rights for adult citizens, "regardless of how ignorant they may be" and "even if they can't vote intelligently." [14] The conception of the equal franchise has evidently been closely tied in with the idea of the equal moral worth of all human beings.

Derivative of the attribution of equal dignity to all persons is the concept of the moral and political infallibility of "the People," the concept of the egalitarian community. As far back as the 1830s, Tocqueville wrote that "the people reign in the American political world as the Deity does in the Universe. They are the cause and the aim of all things, everything comes from them and everything is absorbed in them."[15] Not many years later, one finds Walt Whitman asserting that "the life of the common people is the life of God."[16] In the emotional attachment of Americans to the idea of "the People" there is an affective ground for the ideal of community. Though lacking in specific moral connotations, the idea of "the People" represents united virtue, and in the language of the politics of conscience it is counterposed to the idea of "the interests," who are understood as special groups that either enjoy or seek special place and privilege without any moral claim to it. This language is found in the rhetoric of both major political parties from generation to generation. Interests are self-seeking and manipulative partial groups; "the People" are, by contrast, the moral force of the solidary community. It is probably not too much to say that for a pluralistic and secularizing time, the idea of "the People" functionally fills the role played by "the Church" in Puritan times; it is the community of the saints, the elect. The idea developed at the same moment that Emersonian transcendentalism supplanted Puritan theology as the major language of the American politics of conscience. Just as liberty and the moral commands of the holy community are in perfect harmony in the thought of John Winthrop, so are they fused and harmonized in the thought of Walt Whitman. As Vernon Parrington has paraphrased Whitman's idea: "Not in distinction but in oneness with the whole we find the good life, for in fellowship is love and in the whole is freedom; and love and freedom are the law and the prophets."17

The Politics of Interest

In the American politics of interest, equality does not support liberty. The two are squarely pitted against one another. In the result, individual liberty triumphs; it reins in and severely limits the egalitarian tendencies of the culture.

Property and the Work Ethic

One of Hochschild's young but needy respondents, who earned only $6000 a year in 1976, echoed the Harrington themes of hard work and acquisition. She thought that people could very well make money if they made up their minds not to be lazy. She saw herself as an ambitious achiever, despite her poverty (p. 29). She also expressed Adam Smith's concept of the "unseen Hand" that converts interest into social utility (p. 30).

Respondents at the other end of Hochschild's economic spectrum also celebrated the virtues of free enterprise. A forty-eight-year-old businessman told her how hard work and luck had brought him from a childhood of poverty to the position of a businessman. He was owner of a business that allowed him the luxuries of suburban life, and enabled him to support two children in graduate school (pp. 30–31). He thought welfare payments were bad for the poor, morally corrupting. Welfare taught them to be content with living on a dole rather than to embrace the work ethic (p. 31).

One of Hochschild's needy respondents described the operation of the system of free enterprise as something resembling a Hobbesian war of all against all. "There's always going to be conflict, jealousy.... Everybody's out to beat everybody, and it's just human nature to try to get away with everything you can.... People are fighting each other—it's a good thing. The more he fights, the more rewards he gets" (p. 38). Like that of Hobbes, the conflictual framework of this respondent resembled one of natural physical necessity rather than an institutionalized system of economic order governed by principles of justice.

In the conception of economic freedom under consideration, liberty and equality come together at only one point—in the equal right of all to compete for material well-being. It is significant that in Jefferson's first draft of the Declaration of Independence, the word "property" appeared in place of "the pursuit of happiness." The famous triad of natural rights announced by the Declaration enshrines an equal right of all Americans to personal freedom and security and to compete in the marketplace. That these are introduced in this document as God-given inalienable rights appears to place them in the context of the politics of conscience rather than in the realm of interest politics. But the justification of individual rights with both these languages is characteristic of American political culture. It has also been argued that the religious categories employed by writers like John Locke and his American successors were adopted by the rising middle-class intelligentsia as a useful way to legitimate for all an economic and political system that this new class found personally profitable.[18] Whatever the semantics of the matter, it should be stressed that liberty as free enterprise runs contrary to the norm of equality. It produces social stratification and an elite structure in society.

The overriding importance of liberty as freedom to acquire property is found throughout American history. Despite his political egalitarianism, Jefferson was a free enterpriser, as were his Federalist opponents. Men like James Madison, who helped develop a complicated constitutional system of separated, divided, and balanced authorities, thought that the "first object of government" was to protect "different and unequal faculties of acquiring property." "All men must be free to seek their immediate profit and to associate with others in the process," declared Madison.[19]

And so things have remained, through the creation of the Horatio Alger success myth in the last part of the nineteenth century and down to the present. "There is probably no people on earth," wrote a nineteenth-century immigrant to the United States "with whom business constitutes pleasure, and industry amusement, in an equal degree with the inhabitants of the United States of America."[20]

Contemporary survey research bears out the continued authority of the profit motive for Americans. In a 1979 study, 91 percent of the respondents disagreed with this statement: "The government should limit the amount of money any individual is allowed to earn in a year." And 73 percent supported this proposition: "The profits a company or business can earn should be as large as they can fairly earn." In a 1975–77 study, 54 percent of the public agreed that the profit system teaches the value of hard work and the importance of the drive to succeed, while only 16 percent thought instead that it brings out the worst qualities in people.[21]

The Rejection of Economic Equality
In view of these opinions, it is not strange that when "equality" is translated from the realm of moral estimate and social compassion to the domain of economic activity, it should be denigrated by the American public. In his pioneering study of 1962, Robert Lane found that the blue-collar workers he interviewed had a positive fear of economic equality. The existence of a superintending economic elite gave them a sense of security. Lane's respondents did not sympathize with people lower than them on the economic scale. Nor did they wish themselves to be raised, by government policy, to a level they had not achieved by personal effort. Were a demand for leveling to capture the public mind, they thought it would destroy individual incentive. (They had internalized the work ethic very well.) Lane's subjects had also given up hedonic desires in order to achieve something like middle-class respectability.[22]

In her 1976 update and revision of Lane's study, Hochschild found that the same kinds of attitudes obtained after the passage of fourteen years. One of her needy respondents remarked that the rich must have worked hard for their money, and that they deserved it (p. 112). Here inequality is legitimated by attribution of the work ethic to the successful. Another subject spoke disparagingly of the welfare state for leveling society. This person viewed the system as a "gigantic rip-off" by the lazy. Recipients whose stories he recounted "just want to keep their booze, car, and that's it." The "deserving poor" did not come into his ken (p. 116). In summary, research indicates that the people who support equality in what Hochschild calls "the socializing domain" support economic inequality (p. 118). In specific cases, they usually sought a ground for legitimating differentiation. In viewing the system as a whole, however, they tended to accept it as though it were a fact of nature (pp. 122, 125).

The outright rejection of economic equality by rich and poor alike depicted in Lane's and in Hochschild's reports of their interviews in a specific New England locale has been shown by fifty years of survey research to hold true for the nation as a whole. In 1937 and 1939, in the midst of the Great Depression, only 30 to 35 percent of respondents to national *Fortune* polls supported redistribution of wealth from rich to poor by taxation. Even those in the lowest quarter of the income scale did not favor such a measure by more than 46 percent. Of the unemployed, a bare majority of 54 percent were ready to seek redistribution in 1939, while only 44 percent supported such a view in 1937. When in March 1939 a poll used the word "confiscation" to describe the measure and pitted the individual's freedom to earn against the requirements of the "public good," support for the measure was only half of that registered in the less radically worded poll. This was true for the national average and for the poor and unemployed categories as well.[23]

Polls carried out in 1974 and 1976 yielded results similar to those of forty years earlier. In the 1976 poll, blue-collar workers registered 51 percent of their number in favor of the proposition that "the government should tax the rich heavily in order to redistribute the wealth." Interestingly, only 47 percent of the unemployed held this view, which was also the percentage of the nation as a whole in favor of this position.[24]

Equality and Public Policy

Despite the rejection by a majority of all social groups of absolute equality of condition, there is no question that the American egalitarian tradition, expressed both through the politics of conscience and the politics of interest, has greatly influenced public policy over the generations. The national faith in the equal worth of all human beings has passed over into public measures designed not to produce economic leveling but to ensure broadly defined equality of opportunity for all persons. From the passage of the Thirteenth, Fourteenth, and Fifteenth Amendments to the Constitution down to the civil rights legislation of the 1960s, blacks gradually achieved a large measure of legal, political, and social equality with whites. Here the meaning of "equality" has been interchangeable with the concept of "freedom." Equality of opportunity has meant equal freedom.

Lyndon Johnson's War on Poverty, despite its many administrative failures, gave large numbers of blacks, as well as poor whites, greater equality of economic opportunity than they had ever before enjoyed, and brought millions of blacks and poor whites into the ranks of the middle class. Over roughly the same period, women have achieved greater equality with men.

Large-scale welfare programs like those of the War on Poverty were not intended by their authors to create a permanently dependent class in American society, like that feared by Lane's and Hochschild's respondents. They were aimed instead at developing all Americans into self-reliant, independent persons. As Lyndon Johnson himself described his objective: "The War on Poverty is not a struggle simply to support people, to make them dependent on the generosity of others.... It is a struggle to give (them) a chance."[25] So as one moves from the private world of individual economic endeavor to the world of public economic and social policy, the American view of equality changes once again.

A Positive Role for Government
Despite their fear of economic equality, Lane's subjects in his 1962 study did not, like nineteenth-century exponents of free enterprise or today's libertarian or economic conservative, view government with suspicion. They saw "big government" as working for them. Hochschild's study of 1976 revealed a similar attitude overall, despite some fears for the corrupting effect of welfare programs. One needy respondent, reflecting on the role of government in society, saw government as the protector of private property, but she also wanted the government to prevent property from inflicting great harm on the poor. Like Lane's subjects, she was aware of the reality of private power as a repressive force, and viewed government as a democratic countervalent. Fair prices and salient community needs dominated private rights and community needs for her. And she did not expect this to emerge from the unseen hand of the market. A more progressive tax structure she saw as an important device for establishing this balance. With more tax revenue from the rich, the government could "eliminate college tuition, increase Social Security payments, guarantee job training and jobs with a livable income, and provide national health insurance" (p. 149). When directly confronted with questions of equalizing property, this subject backed off from equality. Yet in considering public policy, she favored redistribution. To bring these divergent lines of thought together she espoused the concept of a guaranteed minimum income, but rejected the idea of putting a ceiling on incomes (p. 151).

Another of Hochschild's needy respondents expressed pessimism about the ability of government to effect redistribution. He saw taxes as high because of graft by politicians. His mind was filled with traditional American stereotypes of government officials as conniving rascals who cannot be trusted, an attitude that served to reinforce his acceptance of economic stratification and to blunt hope for greater equality. He preferred no taxation at all to progressive taxation by a government he could not trust (pp. 152–53). But others of Hochschild's respondents expressed greater optimism about government. The extent of existing equality pleased them, and they were hopeful the egalitarian trend under government auspices would continue (p. 156). Their faith in public redistributive measures was expressed, however, with the qualification that it should extend only to equality of opportunity, not equality of result (p. 158).

Survey research shows that there has been some shift away from support for redistributive welfare programs. James Kluegel and Eliot Smith write that "compared to 1969, the public is now more likely to agree that we are spending too much money on welfare and to deny that people on welfare try to find work to support themselves." Nevertheless, sympathy for those on welfare remains consistently high. And support for guaranteed jobs over the same period showed only a small decline.[26]

Tension between the Politics of Conscience and the Politics of Interest

In measuring the views of her well-to-do subjects on egalitarian policies, Hochschild found tension between principles attached to what is here called the politics of conscience and the principles of the politics of interest, both of which the subjects had internalized. But on margin she found greater support among the rich for more political equality than was dictated by their own material self-interest (p. 165). One of the wealthy subjects opted for guaranteed jobs and public programs of job training. She thought that social security should have a redistributive effect, and she favored tuition subsidies for college students and loans to medical students. In the latter instance, she saw such equalization of opportunity for some as beneficial to the whole society in the long run (p. 166). She also supported national health insurance. But in evaluating the idea of a minimum income, she wondered whether it would be fair to those who had succeeded on their own (p. 167). Another well-to-do subject resolved the tension between freedom and equality by viewing private property as an instrument for the achievement of freedom, though not as an end in itself. And he was ready to entertain the idea of more egalitarian policies to achieve that goal. Overall, the respondent was "less protective of differentiating property rights than many of the poor, and his egalitarianism sometimes dominated his economic self-interest."[27]

Equal Freedom

In concluding her discussion of political egalitarianism, Hochschild found rich and poor respondents alike to be genuinely egalitarian in this domain. "They want tax and social welfare policies mainly to take from the rich and give to the poor and middle classes" (p. 181). Their general attitude seems attributable to the prominent role of the politics of conscience in forming the American mind. They saw equality of rights as directly inferable from the idea of inherent human equality, a basic tenet of conscience (p. 185). Otherwise stated, Americans believe above all in freedom, but in freedom that is equal for all.

Recent survey research finds similar tensions between the politics of conscience and the politics of interest. Kluegel and Smith, in the conclusion to their chapter on redistributive policy, write that "redistribution is opposed if it is believed to take away rewards that are earned by individual efforts and abilities or to reduce incentives that motivate people to work hard." They also found that egalitarian attitudes develop popular support for all sorts of redistributive policies other than welfare. But on the other hand, "Inegalitarianism also influences most policy views, reducing support for all forms of redistribution except government ownership and guaranteed income."[28]

Ethics and Public Policy: Some Case Studies

In an earlier part of this chapter it was observed that the popular politics of conscience and politics of interest are mirrored in systematic ethical systems that are used today to analyze issues of public policy—Kantian and utilitarian ethics. It is now time to review some cases typical of those that come before decision makers and policy analysts in the course of their daily work and see what results from applying the norms of these two schools of ethics to the moral issues involved. In the popular culture there are marked tensions between a politics of conscience and a politics of interest. What is the case in systematic ethical analysis?

The Case of AID and the Single Welfare Mother

A case in the area of welfare policy that revolves around issues of distributive justice was published in the February 1983 issue of the *Hastings Center Report*.[29] It involved a single woman who requested and obtained artificial insemination by donor (AID) from a private physician. The obstetrician examined her for her medical and psychological suitability and obtained letters attesting to her emotional stability and responsibility (in the narrow sense). (This was in keeping with the traditional individualist conception of the patient-doctor relationship, in which the physician's moral responsibility is first and foremost to his patient on a fee-for-service basis.)

A part-time worker, the subject received $161 in monthly pregnancy welfare assistance. After her child's birth, she filed for and obtained $401 monthly in AFDC assistance. According to the report of the case, Ms. S. knew about and planned to obtain welfare benefits before contacting the obstetrician. Indignant members of the community in which she lived thought she ought not to have been artificially inseminated while harboring an intention to obtain public support for herself and her baby. Some even claimed that Dr. F. ought to pay the pregnancy costs. And the physician was concerned that he had contributed to the abuse of the welfare system. Intuitively, these people sensed that something was wrong. Yet there were no legal restrictions on what the obstetrician had done. Were there clear norms in the culture that might have guided his decision? Centrally at issue was the conflict between a woman's right to bear children and society's claim of right to be free of the financial burden implicit in her claim.

When students discussed this case in a seminar at the University of Rochester, they quickly agreed that the obstetrician had no moral responsibility to question Ms. S. about her financial status. His role was seen as restricted to medical questions. Did *society* have such a responsibility, which should have been written into the law? Reasoning by analogy to adoption, it was clear that a demonstration of financial responsibility ought to be required of the prospective parent. But it was also clear that such a requirement rested on a traditional conception of morality. Also, one could question the analogy. Adoption is obviously a privilege, since the prospective parent seeks custody of a child not his or her own, for whom a social agency is acting as guardian. But in the case of AID, the child involved is the claimant's own flesh and blood. Also, the situation is quite new, unlike the petition for adoption. Should it be governed by traditional norms of personal responsibility or by the financial need of the mother?

Reasoning by a different analogy, in the absence of a norm directly applicable to the case, the class concluded that if an unmarried woman is free to become pregnant through casual liaisons, she is free to become pregnant by the use of a scientific process. If society, through its scientific expertise, provided Ms. S. with the device by which she became pregnant, by the provision of the AFDC law, society gives unmarried people the opportunity to cohabit without accepting responsibilities that might follow from cohabitation. No law forbids this, and it appears to be more and more acceptable as traditional taboos on unmarried sex decline and the value of individual freedom takes on new authoritative meanings. While unmarried sex is still frowned on as immoral in some sectors of society, would the act of artificial insemination be as much condemned, since it carries no sexual pleasure with it? Surely, motherhood and childbearing are socially valued things. If these analogies hold, then one would have to ask why the unmarried mother who conceived her child through casual liaisons should morally be entitled to AFDC payments, but the mother via artificial insemination not so entitled. Intentional acts may be involved in *both* cases. When they are not, is carelessness about the possibility of impregnation (which implies irresponsibility) better than intentionality?

Some students in the seminar, admitting that they could not distinguish between the two kinds of cases, concluded that AFDC payments should be denied to *all* unmarried women. In the absence of a clear social norm condemning pregnancy out of wedlock, the warrant for this judgment would be a utilitarian decision that the general pain caused by tax expenditures for the support of illegitimate children and their mothers was greater than the pleasure of mothering and living experienced by the women and children who receive public help. This position was reinforced for these students by their libertarian attachment to norms of individual responsibility.

Within a Kantian frame of reference, one would have to assess the rights of the mothers and children involved to a decent minimum support under the general rubric of the requirements of individual autonomy and social compassion. Reasoning from this basis, it would appear that society would not have a clear moral warrant to deny single women the right to artificial insemination and to public support consequent upon its success. Yet there remained among the students who took this position a sense that somehow society was being put upon, taken advantage of by the individuals involved. Just what can be claimed of society by individuals asserting their rights to autonomous decision about the conduct of their lives? Utilitarian and deontological norms seem here to be directly in conflict with one another, just as Hochschild frequently found them to be in her 1976 study under the guise of differentiating and egalitarian principles. A decision in either direction would necessarily violate the opposite norm.

But there are other relevant considerations. It is clear that the original Kantian idea of individual autonomy and its correlative social obligation of compassionate support rested on the assumption that the claimant of the

right of autonomy was herself a morally responsible person. And the test of
moral responsibility was willingness to engage only in actions that could be
universalized without producing contradictions (the Categorical Impera-
tive). But there is a question whether the behavior of the AID recipient
could be universalized in this case. Universalized, the rule would have to
take the form of a proposition that anyone wishing to enjoy a private value
at public expense would have a right to claim that support. If everyone
acted on this rule, no one would receive any help, for there would be no
revenues in the public treasury. The AFDC law would therefore have to
contain a provision to exclude from its coverage women who do not behave
in a socially responsible way in the use of their reproductive capacities. This
would have the effect of excluding from public support not only AID recipients but all unwed mothers.

It is the case, however, that contemporary definitions of autonomy do
not include the Kantian notion of moral responsibility. One criterion of
autonomy in the language of bioethics today is "competency." And Tom
Beauchamp and James Childress argue that it is commonly thought that

> a person is competent if and only if that person can make decisions
> based on rational reasons [sic]. In biomedical contexts this standard
> entails that a person must be able to understand a therapy or research
> procedure, must be able to weigh its risks and benefits, and must be
> able to make a decision in the light of such knowledge and through
> such abilities.[30]

Nothing is said about the individual's willingness to submit his or her
maxim to the test of universalizability. (In a subsequent section of their
book, Beauchamp and Childress write of "autonomous suicide" and its
criteria. This would be moral nonsense to Kant, who argued that suicide
cannot be universalized in his *Groundwork of the Metaphysics of
Morals*.)[31] Viewed this way, the problem takes the form of a conflict
between a traditional conception of morality and a modern understanding
of individual freedom. In the recent literature of ethics and public policy
one frequently finds arguments calling for the restoration of such traditional
conceptions in the name of the common good.[32]

The Debate about Capital Punishment

After having been proscribed for some years, capital punishment has been
restored for particular offenses. The policy vacillation represented in this

matter is a testimony to strongly opposed opinions in the culture concerning the rightness of state authority taking the lives of convicted criminals. It is interesting, however, that the deontological and the utilitarian position in the matter each has a split personality.

Retributive justice as vengeance ("an eye for an eye") has few vocal supporters among influentials in society. Support for capital punishment these days is registered on one or both of two grounds: (1) that its existence may deter would-be criminals from criminal acts, especially murder (a utilitarian ground); and (2) that capital punishment is required to maintain respect for the law by a rational society (a deontological ground). Kant himself held for capital punishment on the latter basis. In his view, the criminal, as a free rational moral agent, wills his own punishment. In his *Metaphysical Elements of Justice,* Kant writes: "If [a person] has committed a murder, he must die.... There is no substitute that will satisfy the requirement of legal justice." Alternatively, many utilitarians argue that the statistical evidence available does not establish that capital punishment deters; and deontologists, coming at the question from a standpoint of egalitarian compassion, urge that a socially unequal society decrees unequal punishments for people of different social origins. (This embraces the idea that there are many miscarriages of justice because of prejudice and because of the ability of white-collar criminals to influence the justice system, as well as the idea that society is in part responsible for crimes by ghetto people.) Other deontologists, standing on the principle of the sacredness of human life, hold that killing, even by state authority, is never justified.

A new method of utilitarian analysis in the criminal justice field applies economic theory to criminal behavior. "One of the basic predictions [of this theory]," write William A. Luksetich and Michael D. White, "is that an increase in the expected costs of committing crimes would result in a reduction in the amount of crime."[33] On the basis of this reasoning, capital punishment, which exacts the greatest cost, should deter. Luksetich and White, after reviewing the major extant empirical studies of the matter, admit that statistics do not bear out the theory. While there is evidence that the threat of punishment deters, this cannot be said of capital punishment. But the two authors believe that evidence has not yet been collected in a way suitable to an adequate test of their hypothesis. Evidence on hand also does not show the opposite—that the death penalty does *not* deter.

Another writer, who comes at the question both on utilitarian and deontological grounds, is Ernest van den Haag. This theorist argues for the death penalty from the position that it *might* in fact be a deterrent. In an attempt to meet the argument of deontologists who point to the problem of miscarriages of justice, van den Haag pleads that the murder of innocent victims by criminals is also an injustice. He concludes that "the irrevocable injustice sometimes inflicted by the death penalty would not significantly militate against it, if capital punishment deters enough murders to reduce the total number of innocents killed."[34] He points to the deterrent effect of punishment as such and concludes that conscience is probably reinforced by the threat of coercive actions.[35] The obligation to behave lawfully, he claims, "would scarcely be felt if those who do not feel or follow it were not to suffer punishment."[36] From arguments of this sort, added to the hypothesis of empirical researchers such as Isaac Ehrlich that additional executions might reduce the incidence of murder, he concludes that the death penalty *could* cause enough deterrence to be warranted. He thinks it more appropriate to estimate in this direction than to accept victimization of the innocent by murderers. Van den Haag also supports the death penalty with a version of the Kantian argument that capital punishment is called for simply to see that justice is done and the rule of law vindicated. That miscarriages of justice occur he does not think warrants allowing additional injustice to accrue by failing properly to punish acts such as murder.

Hugo Bedau, arguing against the death penalty on purely utilitarian grounds, claims that van den Haag's case is speculative and that no evidence exists that "there is any class of actual or potential criminals for which the death penalty exerts a marginally superior deterrent effect over every less severe alternative."[37] In this important area of criminal justice it is clear that there are not only sharp and deep divisions between deontological and utilitarian positions but that these are also present within each of these rule-bound ethical systems. Does this point to fundamental difficulties within the national ethical sense as well?

Environmental Ethics: The Problem of Short-Run Utilitarianism
A look at the problem of environmental pollution will conclude the case analyses. The problem arises out of a simple conflict between two utilitarian values: prosperity and full employment today versus healthy living associated with environmental integrity in the future. An example is the tension between the welfare of the industries in the Ohio valley, which emit acid-rain-producing smoke, and the health of the forests and lakes of the northeastern United States and eastern Canada. Acid rain is gradually destroying timber stands in the east, as well as all life in numerous lakes.

Political pressures from present economic interests in production and employment have been great enough to prevent legislation to compel a cleanup among the polluting industries that would substantially increase the costs of production. Within private economic calculation, there is no way to factor in long-run social costs of present-day pollution, since efficiency and productivity are computed only for the moment, and with reference to the private profits of particular firms only. And the magic "unseen hand" of the market is not able to produce *future* social well-being. It is possible, however, for analysts to calculate social costs and benefits, and to establish surrogate values for things not traded in a market. There is nevertheless no clear and certain way to give dollar value to social costs that emerge several years down the road. So one may be left with a reduction of the ethical dilemma to purely political terms. Nor have efforts of deontological argument in the literature of environmental ethics, employing rights language with reference to future generations and to nonhuman entities, been more than halting. Is it meaningful to say, for example, that animals and plants have needs and interests, and that ethical status derives from these things? But if species have needs, do not buildings also? Is there *anything* then that would not have moral standing under this rubric?[38] Would a new ethic of the common good that moves away from radically individualist premises help to cope with this dilemma? To develop such an ethic would require not only a break with utilitarianism and deontology. It would demand a rethinking of the fundamentally individualist assumptions of American political culture, the matrix out of which the formal systems of ethical theory proceed.

Summary

In each of the three policy areas examined in this chapter it was noted that strong tensions exist today both within and between the two major schools of ethical reasoning that are especially congenial to the assumptions of American historical political culture. These contradictions have been highlighted in each policy area. It is interesting to observe that during her interviews with the respondents of her New Haven study, Jennifer Hochschild remarked time and time again a sense of bewilderment among her subjects as they became aware that they were contradicting themselves as they moved from one question to another about the meaning and implications of the words "liberty" and "equality" (see especially pp. 29, 31, 33,

34, 238, 240). Hochschild is able to show that some of this confusion results from disjunctions between different universes of discourse rather than from genuine ambivalence. But this is not true throughout; she also found genuine ambivalence and incoherence (p. 258). Also, disjunctions are logical gaps, incoherent judgments.

What is the political result of disjunction and ambiguity among the norms of political culture, as these have appeared in the case analyses? One is the American habit of pragmatic compromise. One writer contends that "in philosophy, Americans accepted the ambiguities and contradictions of the Lockeian tradition. The primacy of sensation and the centrality of the moral sense could flourish at once, as long as each of these theories ... did not push too far."[39] It is a habit Americans have displayed since the earliest days. The Constitution of 1787 is a prime example of its prevalence. It represents a grand compromise, or rather a whole series of them, designed not theoretically but in a practical way to reconcile energy at the center of the political system with liberty in its parts. John Mercer, commenting in 1830 on The Federalist, which aimed at justifying this instrument of government to a diverse people, noted that this work "addresses different arguments to different classes of the American public, in the spirit of an able and skillful disputant before a mixed assembly. Thus from different numbers of this work, and sometimes from the same number, may be derived authorities for opposite principles and opinions."[40] On the other hand, there are kinds of results that are not so happy. Political paralysis in the face of urgent issues is perhaps the most dangerous. Evidence that this is so is presented in other parts of this book.

Notes

1. Samuel Huntington writes that "people sometimes speak of an 'American ideology.' But in the American mind, these ideas do not take the form of a carefully articulated, systematic ideology.... They constitute a complex or amorphous amalgam of goals and values, rather than a scheme for establishing priorities among values and for elaborating ways to realize values." American Politics: The Promise of Disharmony (Cambridge, Mass.: Harvard University Press, 1981), 15.

2. John Winthrop, in his speech to the General Court of Massachusetts Bay Colony, in Vernon L. Parrington, Main Currents in American Thought (New York: Harcourt, Brace, 1930), 1:49.

3. Ralph Barton Perry, *Puritanism and Democracy* (New York: Vanguard, 1944), 354, quoted in Herbert McClosky and John Zaller, *The American Ethos* (Cambridge, Mass.: Harvard University Press, 1984), 65.

4. See John G.A. Pocock, *The Machiavellian Moment* (Princeton: Princeton University Press, 1975).

5. C.B. Macpherson, *The Theory of Possessive Individualism* (London: Oxford University Press, 1962), 175.

6. Ibid., 176, 177.

7. *Time*, 25 May 1987, 14, 27.

8. Ibid., 27.

9. See Jennifer Hochschild, *What's Fair?: American Beliefs about Distributive Justice* (Cambridge, Mass.: Harvard University Press, 1981). It is possible that this study is only regionally valid; however, the national survey findings cited in this chapter appear to show national applicability. Quotations from this book are parenthetically cited.

10. Opinions and Values of Americans Survey, 1975–77, Questions 1 and 3, in McClosky and Zaller, *American Ethos*, 66, table 3-2.

11. See James R. Kluegel and Eliot R. Smith, *Beliefs about Inequality* (New York: Aldine de Gruyter, 1986), 45–48.

12. McClosky and Zaller, *American Ethos*, 70, 71–72.

13. Cited in ibid., 74. See the discussion of this study in William T. Bluhm, *Ideologies and Attitudes: Modern Political Culture* (Englewood Cliffs, N.J.: Prentice-Hall, 1974), 91–95.

14. Civil Liberties Study 1978–79; Political Affiliation and Beliefs Study, 1958; in McClosky and Zaller, *American Ethos*, 75, table 3-6.

15. Alexis de Tocqueville, *Democracy in America*, trans. M. Reeve et al. (New York: Knopf, 1951), 1:58.

16. Quoted in Parrington, *Main Currents*, 2:76.

17. Ibid., 77.

18. See, e.g., Richard Cox, *Locke on War and Peace*, (Oxford: Clarendon Press, 1960); William T. Bluhm et al., "Locke's Idea of God: Rational Truth or Political Myth?" *Journal of Politics*, 42 (May 1980): 414–38.

19. *The Federalist*, No. 10.

20. In McClosky and Zaller, *American Ethos*, 101.

21. Ibid., 120, table 4-5.

22. See the summary and evaluation of Lane's findings in Bluhm, *Ideologies and Attitudes*, 85–87.

23. The question read: "Do you think our government should or should not confiscate all wealth over and above what people actually need to live on

decently, and use it for the public good?" The results of the polls referred to are analyzed in Hochschild, *What's Fair?*, 16–19.

24. Ibid., 18. See also Kluegel and Smith, *Beliefs about Inequality*, 76–81; and Sidney Verba and Gary R. Orren, *Equality in America* (Cambridge, Mass.: Harvard University Press, 1985), 253. This is a study of views toward equality held by a variety of leadership or elite groups in America. Regarding economic equality, these researchers found that "some [leadership] groups want more income equality, but almost none wants complete equality."

25. Quoted in McClosky and Zaller, *American Ethos*, 89. For a capsulized review of public policies directed to redistribution of income toward the poor, see Kluegel and Smith, *Beliefs about Inequality*, 153–54.

26. Kluegel and Smith, *Beliefs about Inequality*, 154–55.

27. Hochschild, *What's Fair?*, 169. Samuel Huntington, in writing of tension in American political culture, describes the phenomenon of "creedal passion" which brings on efforts to bring practice into line with ideals. See his *American Politics*.

28. Kluegel and Smith, *Beliefs about Inequality*, 174, 175.

29. *Hastings Center Report* 13, no. 1 (February 1983): 22. The analysis of this case draws on seminar discussions at the University of Rochester.

30. Tom L. Beauchamp and James F. Childress, *Principles of Biomedical Ethics* (New York: Oxford, 1979), 69.

31. See ibid., 87, 89.

32. See, e.g., Daniel Callahan, "Minimalist Ethics," *Hastings Center Report,* October 1981, 19ff.

33. William A. Luksetich and Michael D. White, *Crime and Public Policy* (Boston: Little, Brown, 1987), 85.

34. "On Deterrence and the Death Penalty," in *Ethics and Public Policy,* ed. T.L. Beauchamp and T.P. Pinkard (Englewood Cliffs, N.J.: Prentice-Hall, 1983), 222.

35. See also Ernest van den Haag, "Is Capital Punishment Just?" Reprint 11, Georgetown University, Ethics and Public Policy Center, September 1978.

36. Van den Haag, "On Deterrence and the Death Penalty," 223.

37. Ibid., 233.

38. See "Preserving Endangered Species," *Report of the Center for Philosophy and Public Policy 5* (Fall 1985).

39. Henry May, in Michael Kammen, *People of Paradox: An Inquiry into the Origins of American Civilization* (New York: Knopf, 1972), 218.

40. Ibid., 219.

CHAPTER 4

American Democracy and the Fragmentation of Consensus

In Western democracies, electorate attitudes and party systems have been expected to provide broad frameworks of preferences within which specific policies can be formulated. Traditionally, parties have been seen as representing coalitions of voters and as facilitating the election of policy makers who would respond to the interests of these coalitions. When these coalitions remained stable, they provided a basis for coherence in governmental policy and a predictable policy environment for the analyst. But in recent years, many scholars contend that democratic electorates have become increasingly volatile and divided, and have been unable to give consistent guidance to public officials. These electorates are in flux, and no one is certain in what direction they are headed. But it is clear that current trends pose important challenges to the political skills of elected officials.

Electoral coalitions have destabilized in the 1970s and 1980s. For reasons discussed below, this is likely to continue well into the 1990s. Changing political currents lead to oscillating policies that can create serious problems for the policy analyst. The environment for coherent analysis becomes kaleidoscopic. The electorate provides little direction for elected officials, and these officials increasingly begin to think in terms of short-term tactical approaches providing meager support, in turn, for policy analysts. In these conditions, short-term political considerations will often override policy analysis.

Current trends portend keen "electoral disorder." If they persist (and they are likely to), the policy analyst must expect to continue to function in an uncertain environment. If electoral stability were again to become the norm, then presumably the analyst would be in a better position to develop and implement rational procedures in decision making. Whatever the future holds, the policy analyst must be aware of electoral realities, since these are exceptionally important constraints on the behavior of elected officials.

The remainder of this chapter focuses on two questions: What is happening in the electorate? What do these developments bode for the future? The bulk of the material is based on information from the American system; however, some important electoral changes have been studied in greater detail in other Western democracies. To treat these trends fully, reference is also made to these non-American studies.

The "New Class" and Postmaterial Values

One major trend that has been postulated in recent years is the emergence of a New Class as the result of postindustrial society. In this view, postindustrial society features expertise and education as key resources and mind work as the dominant form of activity. Those who operate with this paradigm increasingly set the political agenda and structure the acceptable boundaries of political action.[1] One practical outcome of this has been a fracturing of the political party system, which had been based on materialistic economic interests, and a lessening of that system's ability to develop coherent party positions on the issues. The problem is most obvious with the parties of the left, such as the Democrats in the United States, a party described by some as having a "split personality."

New Class Democrats (those who are forty years old and younger, college educated, and in professional and managerial jobs) take issue positions different from those taken by Old Class Democrats (over fifty years of age, without college training, and in blue-collar occupations). New Class Democrats are less interested in the "bread and butter" economic issues than Old Class Democrats. On other questions, they tend to clash with Old Class Democrats. For example, they favor the prochoice position in the abortion controversy, strong environmental protection, racial equality, and freer sexual relations. New Class Democrats are liberal on the so-called social or life-style issues, while Old Class Democrats are conservative on these issues. The result is a deep ideological split within the Democratic party.[2] If the Democrats select someone perceived as liberal on life-style issues (such as George McGovern), the party stands to lose the support of the Old Class Democrats. At the same time, through the various reforms that have opened the party to "democratic" influence, the New Class has considerable power to structure the party's official positions. The result has been that the Democrats have difficulty holding this presidential coalition together.

It is not only the Democratic party that faces problems as a result of this new class division. William S. Maddox and Stuart A. Lilie argue that the terms *liberal* and *conservative* are no longer clear guides to the political positions of Americans.[3] They contend that at least two separate issue dimensions are needed to categorize individuals' ideological positions (table 2 illustrates): government intervention in the economy and expansion of personal freedom. Juxtaposing these dimensions results in four ideological groupings.

Table 2. Matrix of Ideological Types

		Government Intervention in the Economy	
		FAVOR	OPPOSE
Expansion of Personal Freedom	FAVOR |	Liberal	Libertarian
	OPPOSE |	Populist	Conservative

Those who favor government intervention in the economy and expansion of personal freedoms are liberals in this scheme; conservatives favor less government intervention in the economy and are not in favor of expanding personal freedoms; populists are for government involvement in the economy but against expanding life-style freedoms; libertarians are against government intervention in the economy but favor expansion of personal freedom. The net result is *two* national parties with split personalities.

Self-identified Democrats tend to be largely liberals and populists (the two factions correspond somewhat to the New Class-Old Class distinction already discussed). Republicans, in contrast, are largely conservative and libertarian. Voting behavior is clearly affected by which stance one adopts. Libertarians voted for Nixon, Ford, and Reagan from 1972 to 1980, and conservatives did the same. Populists supported Nixon, then Carter twice. Finally, liberals supported McGovern and Carter twice. Through the mid-1980s, a libertarian-conservative alliance has managed to survive. This relationship is likely to continue *if* economic issues dominate political campaigns. Alternatively, if life-style or social issues become dominant, the Republicans may find their apparently powerful coalition splitting in a manner similar to the fate of the Democrats in 1972. In that year, populists deserted the Democrats because McGovern was seen as too liberal on social issues; at the same time, New Class liberals found his social liberalism to their liking. To date, however, the inherent tension within the ranks of the Republican party has not proved to be a particularly great problem.

Exactly what kinds of people make up the various ideological categories? Maddox and Lilie note that liberals are younger (under forty-one), have some college education, are less religious or are Jewish, come from all income levels, and are from the Northeast and West. Populists are the New Deal generation or older, have a high school education (or less), make relatively little money, are working class in background, and are 24 percent nonwhite. Conservatives are the people who came of political age in the 1950s or earlier; they come from all educational levels, are middle to upper income, and almost completely white. Finally, libertarians are—simply—the Yuppies. They are under forty-one, have college degrees, earn middle to high incomes, are largely white, and are not religious. The liberals and libertarians are the two fastest-growing segments of the voting electorate. Populists have already begun to decline as a proportion of the electorate. They are, literally, dying out, to be replaced by liberals and libertarians. While conservatives retain their share of the electorate, they are an aging group too, and the "death effect" will shortly begin depleting their numbers. Currently, however, the rather even electoral division among these four ideological perspectives has introduced an element of instability into partisan politics that could last for the next couple of decades.

The origins and rise of the New Class are important because much research suggests that it is part of the electoral change affecting most of the Western democracies. The most persuasive explanation for the rise of the New Class is Ronald Inglehart's needs theory.[4] He argues that people growing up in a time of scarcity tend to develop "materialist" attitudes. They are so concerned with survival needs—food, shelter, clothing—that they see government's primary responsibility to be the provision of these basic material items. Those who mature in times of abundance, however, such as have existed in the Western world since World War II, take the satisfaction of basic economic and material needs for granted. They instead view government and politics as vehicles for self-expression, for advancing their opportunities for self-development and fulfillment. They are the postmaterialists.

Inglehart offers two basic propositions to explain these trends:

1. *A scarcity hypothesis.* An individual's priorities reflect the socioeconomic environment: One places the greatest subjective value on things that are in relatively short supply.

2. *A socialization hypothesis.* The relationship between socioeconomic environment and value priorities is not one of immediate adjustment; a substantial time lag is involved, for to a large extent, one's basic values reflect the conditions that prevailed during one's pre-adult years.[5]

Findings indicate that younger people and those who grew up in more wealthy homes are most likely to be postmaterial in their orientations—in the United States, Great Britain, France, West Germany, the Scandinavian countries, and even Japan. On political issues, they are more sympathetic to women's rights, efforts to ameliorate poverty, environmentalism, the antinuclear movement, and, in general, life-style freedom. Furthermore, postmaterialists are less likely to accept traditional values. Their orientation is secular and agnostic. For them, God has little importance. They accept homosexuality and sexual permissiveness and prefer easy divorce. In contrast, the materialists are *most* likely to accept traditional values. Inglehart says that it is "precisely those who experience the least economic and physical security in their lives, that have the greatest need for the guidance and reassurance that familiar cultural norms and absolute religious beliefs provide."[6]

Chapter 3 discusses two core value orientations in American thought: a politics of interest and a politics of conscience. At one level, these concepts seem applicable to the conflict between materialists and postmaterialists. Materialists emphasize government's responsibility to focus on economic issues. Liberals, on this issue, want government to ensure minimum wages, fair treatment of workers, and generous unemployment compensation. Conservatives prefer government to carry out policies to enhance the profitability of market enterprises. Either way, there is a preoccupation with securing and advancing material, economic benefits. Self-interest is the underlying motive.

Postmaterialists are somewhat more difficult to categorize, since there are elements of both the politics of interest and of conscience in their belief structures. Clearly, a politics of conscience grounded in a sense of the common good and a commitment to equality is an important component of the postmaterialist orientation. Postmaterialists want government to allow free expression for all (a key part of the politics of conscience). In practical policy terms, postmaterialist individuals support racial and gender equality, and the environment. Their sympathy for these positions reflects their belief that individuals, at one level, should subordinate their narrow self-interest to a greater good. On the other hand, as individuals, this element of the electorate practices and strongly supports a self-centered life style.

Although, as long as the economy stays relatively healthy, there appears to be an inexorable movement toward postmaterialism, the postmaterial successor generation will not be a majority for at least a generation. Materialists will outnumber postmaterialists in Western Europe and the United States in the year 2000, even under the assumptions most favorable to the rise of postmaterialism. Nonetheless, postmaterialists, because they are more politically active, will have considerable ability to shape the political agenda. Paul Abramson and Inglehart note that "since post-materialists will remain a minority, they will often be on the losing side of many political conflicts. Thus, the growth of post-materialism could lead to a growing number of disaffected, but articulate and politically active Europeans, increasing the potential for political protest."[7] Postmaterialists will continue to have agenda-setting power but not effective governing power. Thus, those responsible for governmental policy in the industrialized democracies may expect to face increasing conflict and division in their electorates.

The effects of these changes for the policy analyst will be direct and tangible. In the Federal Republic of Germany, postmaterialists are most skeptical of the North Atlantic Treaty Organization (NATO), are most opposed to nuclear weapons in their country, and are more likely to place themselves in the political left. Jane Y. Junn concludes that "increasingly more educated, active, and politically powerful individuals opposing nuclear weapons deployment will soon be in a position to disagree with, and disrupt, current NATO strategic policy."[8] This obviously has powerful relevance for American foreign policy in the future. Those who undertake policy analysis related to foreign policy must monitor the electoral configurations behind the government policies of other nations if their recommendations are to be useful.

The extent of one's materialism or postmaterialism is affected by economic conditions at a particular point in time (referred to as "period effects" by students of public opinion). One important finding, based on studies of Western European countries from 1970 to 1982, is that the inflation rate has an effect on the degree to which individuals are materialist or postmaterialist (see figure 2).

For each "generation," as the inflation rate goes up, postmaterial values diminish. It is also clear that each successively younger generation has grown more postmaterial than its older age cohorts. In the United States, there may be a considerable irony in these changes. The public gives

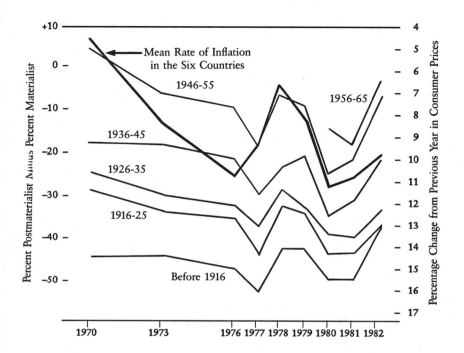

Figure 2. Cohort Analysis of Values of West European Publics, with Inflation Rate in Each Year Shown. From Ronald Inglehart, "The Persistence of Materialist and Post-Materialist Value Orientations," *European Journal of Political Research* 11 (March 1983): 81–91.

the Reagan administration credit for having cooled down inflation. But the administration's success in controlling inflation may have in turn encouraged an upward boost in postmaterialism—a development that could have worked *against* that administration's more conservative principles and its advocacy of a return to traditional values. The result may well be an increased instability in American electoral politics that parallels that emerging in Western Europe.

Findings from a wide variety of studies indicate that the emerging postmaterialist generation has begun to cause political dealignment (a weakening of party ties in the electorate) in many European democracies. Voting and issue views are increasingly shaped by whether one is material or postmaterial in orientation. Nevertheless, European parties continue to be largely based on the more materialist tradition of social class. The result is a

poor fit between the perspectives of postmaterialist voters and the socioeconomic class bases of political party support.

This disjunction is one of the reasons for the development of "Green"
parties in Western Europe. Postmaterialists are not satisfied with the traditional parties of the left. These parties continue to emphasize material issues
relevant to the interests of the working class and their poorer constituents—precisely the issues deemed less important by postmaterialists. As
one response, these voters have moved to support newer "Green" parties in
a number of countries, such as West Germany and the Scandinavian states.
But in the United States at this time, there are really no viable alternatives to
the Democratic and Republican parties. Thus the Republicans have been
able to do reasonably well with younger, postmaterial voters (i.e., the
"libertarians").[9]

But these voters are not likely to stay on board the Republican ship if
traditional values are emphasized in the implementation of public policy. In
the long run, there can be a sorting out of the ideological strains currently in
evidence. But in the short run, the tension within the party systems of the
Western democracies will continue. In the United States, more specifically,
the longer-term future may well be one dominated by liberals versus libertarians, with residual numbers of populists, conservatives, moderates, and
those who are nonideological. For the next twenty years or more, though,
there will likely be continuing instability among the factions within the two
American political parties.

What Have You Done for Me Lately?

Over the past decade, commentators have spoken of a new and invidious
source of individualism in the United States. Christopher Lasch's *Culture of
Narcissism* and Robert Bellah et al.'s *Habits of the Heart* have depicted this
as cancerous in its rejection of common interests and values. Individuals
take advantage of opportunities in order to further their self-interest. The
effort to improve themselves and advance their interests obscures the larger
social context. Pursuit of economic self-interest or self-fulfillment reduces to
a minimum any inherent concern for the larger interests of society. In many
respects, this characterizes the basic motivation of contemporary materialist
and postmaterialist citizens and their representative interest groups and
places them squarely within the politics of interest.

In terms of elections, this new individualism engenders a "What have you done for me lately?" calculus by voters. If incumbents are seen as not having done well, people will vote against them. Samuel Kernell notes that in the Western democracies, people increasingly do not vote *for* candidates; they are more likely to vote *against* them.[10] Indeed, there is evidence that negative voting routinely takes place in the United States. People want quick answers to sometimes difficult problems; if such responses are not forthcoming, they oust the incumbent administration and try again. In times of economic difficulty, like the 1970s, the predictable result will be governmental instability. No policy guides for the future are provided by such voting—only approval or disapproval of past performance. The policy analyst working in Jimmy Carter's Environmental Protection Agency would have had to switch gears dramatically to function in the agency in Ronald Reagan's early administration. This hardly provides the conditions for rational, future-oriented policy on the environment.

The increasingly short-term orientation of the electorate has an impact on candidates for office. For Congress, as noted below, this sensitivity to the electorate leads toward increased errand running and constituency service and away from developing a coherent policy orientation. For presidential candidates, it may encourage overselling of inflated promises on which delivery is improbable or impossible.

Kernell quotes Henry Kissinger as saying:

> There is the problem that as the pressures of their electoral process have increased, governments have become more and more tactically oriented. The more tactically oriented they are, the more short-term their policies. The more short-term their policies, the less successful they are. So we have the paradox that governments following public opinion polls begin to look more and more incompetent.[11]

Examining the electoral politics of Western democracies, including Australia, France, Great Britain, the United States, Japan, and the Federal Republic of Germany, Kernell contends that similar processes exist in all these countries. Assuming that these societies will continue to face chronic economic problems, he argues that candidates for high office will try to outpromise one another about their abilities to turn the economy around. Once in office, however, the winner will be unable to carry out those promises. Hence the leader (and his or her party) will be discredited and ousted at the next election—to be replaced by the leader of the opposition party, who will also have overpromised results.

As the scenario unwinds, voters become increasingly disenchanted. They no longer vote *for* candidates to leadership positions; they now vote *against* incumbents. As economic conditions remain unstable, governments will have to endorse austerity measures, which in turn will lead to greater mass discontent. Kernell concludes that "about all the new austerity offers modern capitalist democracies ... is elite conflict, on occasions ideological stridency, and regime instability."[12]

In the United States, presidential popularity makes a difference in the balance of political power. This is one resource that can assist a President in getting his policy initiatives approved by Congress. But what helps to shape the level of popularity? If Kernell is right, judgments about a President's performance—tied to real-world events—ought to predict people's approval for a President better than abstract values. In an important essay, Charles W. Ostrom and Dennis M. Simon develop a statistical model to explain and predict presidential popularity. They consider the role of unexpected events, legislative success of a President's program, the degree of tension with the Soviet Union, people's judgments about the state of the economy, existence of war, and a honeymoon effect (a boost in Presidents' standing after elections or some sympathy-evoking event, such as an assassination attempt). Each of the above factors, in fact, affects mass approval of the President. "Thus, ... public assessments of presidential performance are anchored in the real world,"[13] and judgments made by a nearsighted electorate become important components of presidential power.

Nor are these findings contradicted by Ronald Reagan's "Teflon effect," for the data do not support its existence. Providing a month-by-month prediction of Reagan's approval ratings, Ostrom and Simon anticipated his levels of approval quite accurately—based on data derived from other Presidents' tenure in the office. For instance, as the economy declined in 1981 and 1982, so did the President's job performance rating, as it has done for other chief executives. When the economy improved and foreign policy crises occurred (with the concomitant "rally 'round the flag" effect), Reagan's approval rebounded. In short, there was nothing mysterious about mass response to the President. It was based largely on assessments by the public of his job performance.

Analysis of data covering 1952 through 1980 suggests a number of points about presidential elections that indicate the growing salience of the "What have you done for me lately?" orientation in the electorate. Over this period, incumbents have been increasingly evaluated on the basis of their past performance. Nonincumbents across the board are more likely to be judged on the basis of expected performance. Performance consistently has outweighed policy as a predictor of electoral support. The only exception over this period was the 1964 Johnson-Goldwater election, which had a strong policy mandate component (1972 had some of this, but to a much lesser extent). This is significant because policy questions are more likely to deal with long-term considerations, while performance factors tend to be tied to short-term voter satisfaction. The Carter-Reagan contest of 1980 is normally viewed as a straightforward retrospective judgment—and rejection—of the performance of incumbent Jimmy Carter; there is little evidence of a policy mandate for Reagan, although the American public was moving in a more conservative direction. The 1984 Reagan-Mondale race featured a retrospective judgment (positive in this case) on Reagan's performance, as did the Bush-Dukakis 1988 election.[14]

In congressional elections, there is a very strong retrospective element. Voters reward incumbents for the services they render. As long as incumbents bring home the pork, serve as ombudsmen, and take credit for government projects, voters will continue to support them. As chapter 5 indicates, this has been an American tradition of long standing, and legislators are aware of its importance.

Retrospective voting creates pressures to do what it takes to get the public to see that an incumbent has done something for them lately. Short-term (or tactical) decision making that overwhelms long-term considerations may result. There is some evidence, for example, that in presidential and majoritarian parliamentary systems, manipulation of the economy may be timed to coincide with elections. Thus national leaders tend to "juice up" the economy just before elections and then try to "cool" it down afterward. Under these conditions, policy analysts in budget offices will discover pressures to subordinate a long-range budgetary approach to the short-term fiscal manueuvers of their political superiors.[15]

Realignment, Dealignment, or What?

Realignment is a shift in coalitions that has pushed the parties into a new, stable alignment. Associated with realignment is the development of a new political agenda and a new set of programs and policies. Has the United States experienced one recently? Is it experiencing one now? How these questions are answered helps sketch the picture of the political future. Affirmative answers to these questions can also provide the policy analyst with a sense that there will be greater stability in the decision-making environment and in institutions than there has been recently. If realignment is not in sight, however, electoral volatility and policy instability will continue as political figures try to appease a public that provides no direction. Across many Western democracies, *something* is happening; it is not yet clear, though, exactly what it is.[16]

Some claim that 1964 (or even 1968) was a critical election year in the United States, one in which the racial issue brought about significant change in political coalitions. This argument sees the following events as linked to the critical nature of the 1964 election.[17]

1. From the 1940s until 1964, Republicans were more moderate and Democrats more conservative in House of Representatives and Senate votes on civil rights bills. After 1964, Democrats in Congress became more moderate to liberal than Republicans in this area.
2. Voters picked up on this. They correctly perceived that the Democrats had become the more liberal party on civil rights.
3. There seems to have been a resulting differentiation between new Democratic and new Republican identifiers after 1964—with new Republicans more conservative and new Democrats more liberal on racial issues.

This chain of events could help explain the defection from the Democratic party of blue-collar workers and southern whites, both groups that are conservative on racial issues.

In the South, there is a large-scale movement away from the Democratic party by whites. This appears to be part of a two-stage process: *First,* southern whites come to see themselves as less Democratic. (Their party identification as Democrats weakens, fewer vote for Democratic presidential candidates, and there is increasing support for Republican candidates in subpresidential races.) This describes a dealigning process "in which traditional party coalitions dissolve without new party coalitions being formed to take their place."[18] A major reason for this change is the rapid loss of Democratic identification in young white voters (much of which occurred between 1964 and 1968). There has been a weakening of Democratic loyalties among many older white voters as well. *Second,* there has been a recent shift toward Republican identification. In 1980 and 1981, for instance, dramatic shifts toward the Republican party occurred among whites in Florida. The key group, once more, was younger voters, with a smattering of older conservative-segregationist Democrats joining the rush. Additionally, many southern whites seem to carry a kind of "dual" identification. They see themselves as Republicans in national elections (President and Congress) and as Democrats in state and local elections. This dual identification seems to have begun developing in, as one might have guessed, 1964.

Available data may fit the pattern of what Reagan pollster Richard Wirthlin calls a "rolling realignment:"

> [A rolling realignment] begins by the electorate ... saying the old agenda does not work, it does not provide help to the poor, it is a burden to the middle class, it is not providing the strength we need in this world, and it is not dealing with inflation. Attitudes change. Second, you get the emotional commitment to party. The third step would be the legal change, namely a shift in party registration. And the fourth step would be picking up the real political power in the grassroots which are state legislatures, Congress, sheriffs, courthouses. We are not to that stage yet.[19]

Key groups in this process, occurring now according to Wirthlin, are white southerners, blue-collar workers, and young voters, all of whom have become more Republican recently.

These studies tend to locate the important election period as 1964–68. Race is apparently part of the answer as to why change has occurred. So, too, is dissatisfaction with Democratic presidential performance. The case for realignment, thus laid out, seems fairly persuasive.

Nonetheless, other aspects of electoral change suggest that the stability of voter realignment may not be great. Both parties have experienced a weakening of voter loyalties that is part of a general weakening of the partisanship in the electorate. For this reason, Martin Wattenberg refers to the erstwhile realignment as "hollow." Political parties seem to be less salient and important to voters.[20] Evidence suggests that much of the gain in Republican identification is performance based, a function of Ronald Reagan's successes as President. In an increasingly candidate-centered age, party does not have the same value as a cue for the electorate as it used to. Furthermore, the greatest shift from Democratic to Republican identification seems to be among the least educated—those who are the least interested and informed politically and, consequently, the most volatile in their views.[21]

The role of the media in influencing the electorate must also be taken into account. Candidates have come to rely more heavily on the media than the party in their campaigns. Data gathered during the 1978 congressional elections indicate that as media spending increases, the candidate becomes more salient to the voters than his or her party. Candidates are becoming electoral entrepreneurs rather than partners on a political team linked by a common party. Moreover, media affect voters' behavior in other ways. Reliance on television as a news source leads to an inability to distinguish candidates' positions and, as a result, reduces voting turnout rates, since those who cannot see differences between candidates are less likely to vote. More generally, greater dependence on television for news is associated with less political knowledge and lower levels of participation, and, paradoxically, the effects are greatest for those with the most education. Television news is considered by people as the most trustworthy, dependable source of what is going on. Television-induced lower levels of political interest and information may be reducing the ability of Americans to judge parties and candidates and, as a result, rendering the electorate more volatile.

These trends indicate that election outcomes will probably depend more and more on the short-term effects of candidate evaluation and on specific issues of concern to relatively small numbers of lightly motivated voters than on the long-term force of party identification. Wattenberg notes:

> even if the Republican surge is a long-lasting one, it will be of limited importance as long as partisanship in the electorate continues to decline. Given the most ideal conditions for party revitalization in decades, all that occurred [in 1984] was a stabilization of the decline. With an incumbent unable to run again, and with what will most likely be fractious campaigns for the presidential nomination within both parties, it seems likely that the conditions in 1988 will be such as to foster further party decline. The candidate-centered age will be with us for a long time to come, regardless of whether the next political era will be a Democratic or Republican one.[22]

Furthermore, much of the debate over realignment in the United States ignores the value changes that seem ongoing as postmaterialism gains and as liberals/libertarians become more numerous at the expense of conservatives/populists. Although Republicans are surely benefiting now from the changes that are occurring, there is no solid evidence of firm electoral stability yet. Identification with party is still weak, and party programs cover potentially uneasy coalitions. If there is to be a stable mass realignment of the "traditional" kind, it is still in the future.

"What have you done for me lately?" will probably remain the key question asked by contemporary individualists. Instability and volatility are likely to remain dominant. If there is or has been realignment, it seems fated to be hollow for the next decade or so. There is unlikely to be the stability needed to maximize the usefulness of policy analysis in areas in which values conflict, although in certain technical areas (e.g., water resources or traffic planning) the analyst may remain unaffected. Short-run, tactical needs of politicians will continue to dominate and remain a part of the landscape within which the policy analyst labors.

The Party Organization: Resurrection or Requiem?

As voters have become less politicized and less oriented toward party, the conclusion of many students of American parties has been that these organizations have gone into decline. Party decline is a source of anguish to political thinkers, many of whom contend that the parties are the only viable mechanism for organizing political discourse in the United States. The two parties, by competing with one another for votes, present alternatives to the citizenry and thus help to structure debate and, ultimately, policy. The decline of party organization, then, is lamented as making the American system more susceptible to interest-group influence.

Frank J. Sorauf, in fact, claims that the likeliest future of electoral politics is individual-candidate-centered and interest-group-sponsored candidacies, with some residual influence of the political party.[23] Ultimately, this course of events would render the electorate even more volatile and make still less likely stable electoral majorities. This would introduce further uncertainty into policy making, with short-term political considerations becoming more important for elected officials as they jockey for position to gain the support of groups. The prospects for rational decision making aided by policy analytic techniques are hardly promising under the gloomier projections.

Some scholars argue that party organizations—at all levels of government—are making a spirited comeback. At the local level, county parties have strengthened organizationally from 1964 to 1980. County parties are more active in fund raising, in distributing campaign literature, in arranging political events, and in voter registration drives, although there is little budgetary support for the local parties and few have even part-time staff to operate their organizations on a day-to-day basis. At the state level, there has been a striking increase in the strength of party organizations. From the 1960s through the 1980s, more and more state parties developed permanent headquarters, hired professional, full-time leadership staff with increasingly specialized staff operations, had state party budgets increase, and began to operate party programs—either directed at building the organizations further or at assisting party candidates in campaigns. Researchers have noted that the Republicans have progressed much more rapidly than the Democrats in these areas. Thus, although both parties at the state level are much stronger organizationally than in 1960, the Republicans have clearly outpaced the Democrats in this respect.[24]

At the national level, there have also been changes toward strengthened parties. The U.S. Supreme Court has recognized the power of the national party organization to make rules that must be adhered to by state government (*Democratic Party* v. *LaFollette*, 1981). Both parties—but, once more, especially the Republicans—have become much more ambitious in their fund-raising efforts. The party organizations collect funds and then disburse them to specific candidates for office or to some state party organizations. They even purchase advertising time on television for generic commercial campaigns on behalf of the party.

On the face of it, parties seem to be coming back and are increasingly able to play the role that democratic theorists have consistently advocated for them. But some problems remain. One case study of the Pittsburgh-area party organizations found that the party activists are not really party loyalists as much as supporters of particular candidates or party leaders. Indeed, many activists are trying to advance their personal ambitions through party involvement.[25] And even though national party organizations are donating money to candidates for office, the party contributions are dwarfed by the influx of political action committee (PAC) money.

Despite the problems just noted, the venerable American parties may well be evolving into important shapers of policy debate. Stronger party organization might help to introduce some order into the present electoral uncertainty. First, as noted above, party organizations at all levels of government have become more vital institutions recently. They are, simply, more *capable* of affecting the structure of policy debate.

Second, party organizations seem to be working toward creating more of a "team" sense and developing greater party unity. In 1978 and 1980, the Republican party's various national organizations (Republican National

Committee and both the Senate and House Republican Campaign Committees) targeted aid for candidates at all levels of government who needed help and who had a chance of victory. The national Republicans also paid for television advertisements extolling the Republican party and its candidates for office ("Vote Republican! For a change!"). The ads seem to have helped improve somewhat Americans' image of the Republican party. These effects could lead to increased power of the national party over those candidates beholden to it for assistance. This might translate into more party influence on elected officials' decision-making behavior. Other evidence shows that party voting in Congress has been increasing since 1968; that is, increasingly Republican members of Congress vote against Democrats, with fewer party crossover votes (technically, party cohesion has been increasing on congressional votes). This may be a measure of the parties' increasing potency as an influence on policy debate and decision.[26]

Third, party organizations—by working hard at getting out the vote on election day—can affect election outcomes (and hence render party candidates more beholden to the organizations). Activities by county parties accounted for about 7 percent of the vote in 1984 in selected statewide and national elections. That is a substantial independent impact—one that could easily affect winning and losing.[27]

These three points together paint an overall picture of a somewhat revitalized party structure (especially Republican organizations) influencing voters and elected officials. At this point, there is evidence that party organizations may be serving to bring some order back into the policy process; it is premature to say anything stronger, given the apparently deep and pervasive roots of the electoral division and volatility described earlier in this chapter.

The Policy Process

An understanding of the trends and relationships within the electorate is important to explaining and predicting the movement of the policy process on issues. Studies indicate that voters' beliefs and the positions of the political parties are in a general sense influential in moving issues onto the government's agenda. For example, based on interviews of policy makers in the areas of health and transportation, John W. Kingdon found that 57 percent of his sample believed that public opinion generally had played an important agenda-setting role; 30 percent thought elections had been significant;

and 29 percent saw parties as being important.[28] These findings indicate that citizens—through their votes, opinions, and/or parties—can have an effect on the first stage of the formal policy process. This fact makes the existence or threat of electoral "disorder" that much more significant in terms of its eventual effects on public policy.

The postmaterialist phenomenon in the electorate has weakened the parties. At the same time, the power of interest groups, especially single-issue interest groups, has grown in the policy process at the agenda-setting stage. In Kingdon's study, interest groups were seen as important in getting issues onto the agenda in almost three-fourths of the case studies examined, and over 80 percent of those interviewed saw them as politically influential. These findings indicate that groups have significantly more impact at the agenda-setting stage than do political parties, elections, or public opinion in general. The problem posed for the policy maker and the policy analyst by these developments stems from the narrowness of group orientations, which is in turn reinforced by postmaterialist views among the electorate. Parties, in their representation of sizable aggregations of electorate preferences, retained the power to move issues through the policy process. Their weakening has meant that issues are now brought to the agenda by interests capable of gaining public and official notice but rarely capable of maintaining sustained support throughout the policy-making process. Analysts can provide useful explanations of the plight of the homeless or the effects of acid rain, and interests can make sufficient public outcry to obtain legislative notice of these problems. But movement toward effective remedial action remains at the mercy of the demands and maneuvers of many other interests, who have other priorities that command official support.

Title I of the 1965 Elementary and Secondary Education Act (ESEA) provides but one example of this phenomenon. Proposed by those interested in improving the education of the disadvantaged, the statute was actually passed by a coalition of interests that constructed a vaguely worded law. Implementation of the statute became, not a question of following congressional mandate, because there was no clear legislative mandate, but instead a matter of each interest dipping into the funding for its own purposes. The result was a thorough undermining of the intentions of those who originally proposed the legislation.

The policy process has become an obstacle course composed of both procedural and substantive pitfalls. In this respect, the disorientation of the electorate is mirrored in the fragmentation of the legislative and executive branches. Difficult decisions in these branches require majority coalitions of some duration, for victory at one point may only increase the intensity of the opposition at the next. Charles O. Jones argues:

> The result is a system of layers of numerical majorities in elections, in referenda, in committee action, in roll-call voting, in court decisions. It is true, of course, that pluralities are sometimes accepted, but it is also true that those who rely on pluralities are likely to be limited in their exercise of authority and subject to criticism.[29]

The divisive effects of the electorate in the decision-making process were demonstrated graphically in the Senate's consideration of President Nixon's family assistance program to reform the welfare system. Representative Wilbur Mills was twice able to put together sufficient support in the House of Representatives to obtain passage. Both times, however, the ideological disagreements in the Senate produced a three-way division that stymied the bill's supporters from putting together a majority for passage. These differences reflected closely three of the four electorate divisions described by Maddox and Lilie. One grouping (populist) supported the measure; another (conservative) opposed it as too generous; the third (liberals) saw the plan as too restrictive on the rights of the poor.[30]

Alternatives designed to circumvent the difficulty of fashioning majorities on policies focus on weakening the wording of legislation so as not to offend anyone deeply or on distributing benefits so broadly that most of the legislators can anticipate advantages for their constituents. The first approach contains the seeds for trouble at the implementation stage, since the vagueness of the policy package leaves little guidance for the supervising agencies. The result, as in the case of the ESEA, discussed above, tends to be an unraveling of the program by a variety of interests adept at exploiting the legislature's vagueness in their favor. In the second instance, resources can be spread so thinly that the program is nowhere effective. Thus, in the case of the Model Cities program under the Johnson administration, legislative support had to be purchased with promises of funds from the program to the point that the program's administrators were simply unable to provide the kind of concentrated aid envisioned by the authors of the legislation. In fact, the Model Cities program is an excellent example of the difficulties that can arise from utilizing advisers with little familiarity with the policy process to formulate major programmatic efforts.

The implementation phase of the policy process has always been fertile ground for interests to exploit the waning of public commitment to programs. In some cases, it may be possible to construct coalitions of sufficient durability to enact reasonably precise policy, but, over the long term, public interest will dissipate while the interests directly affected by the policy will remain. Obviously, if the electorate is moving more markedly toward a self-centered individualism, there will be even less sustained support for administrators attempting to advance broad public purposes. Again, Jones touches on the kind of environment created by contemporary electoral conditions.

> A weakened presidency, a more pretentious Congress, a steady Court, an expanding bureaucracy, enfeebled political parties, disinterested voters, burgeoning group activity, and a changing governmental policy structure—these developments both reflect and contribute to the social change that has characterized recent decades. Anthony King concludes that "American politics has become, to a high degree, atomized." Majorities must still be gathered, but it is much more difficult to build a lasting coalition.[31]

In this context, administrators can be expected naturally to seek security and certainty in the support of the organized interests affected by their programs.

The lack of consensus on basic values in the electorate and the emergence of a narrow, subjective form of individualism among citizens have serious consequences for the policy analyst, whose attachment to careful, rational approaches to issues constitutes the core of his or her occupational calling and, perhaps, orientation toward life. The immediacy of the needs expressed by the electorate pushes the policy analyst toward incremental policy making. He or she must be sensitive to the quickly changing attitudes of a volatile electorate and will find the cautious, small steps of the incremental approach to issues wiser than solutions requiring long-term commitments. Moreover, the fragmented character of the institutions of the policy process in many instances make this stance one of necessity rather than preference.

Notes

1. Everett Carll Ladd, *Where Have All the Voters Gone?* 2d ed. (New York: Norton, 1982).

2. James Q. Wilson, *American Government* (Lexington, Mass.: Heath, 1980), 116–21.

3. William S. Maddox and Stuart A. Lilie, *Beyond Liberal and Conservative* (Washington, D.C.: Cato Press, 1984).

4. Ronald Inglehart, "The Persistence of Materialist and Post-Materialist Value Orientations," *European Journal of Political Research* 11 (March 1983): 81–91; Ronald Inglehart, *Culture Shift* (Princeton: Princeton University Press, 1990).

5. Ronald Inglehart, "Intergenerational Change in Politics and Culture" (paper presented at American Political Science Association meeting, New Orleans, 1985), 2.

6. Ibid., 11.

7. Paul Abramson and Ronald Inglehart, "Generational Replacement and Value Change among the Western European Public" (paper presented at Midwest Political Science Association Meeting, Chicago, 1985), 21.

8. Jane Y. Junn, "German Post-Materialism" (paper presented at International Society of Political Psychology meeting, Toronto, 1984).

9. Russell J. Dalton, Scott C. Flanagan, and Paul Allen Beck, eds. *Electoral Change in Advanced Industrial Democracies* (Berkeley: University of California Press, 1984).

10. Samuel Kernell, "Strategy and Ideology" (paper presented at American Political Science Association meeting, Washington, D.C., 1980).

11. Ibid., i.

12. Ibid., 38.

13. Charles W. Ostrom and Dennis M. Simon, "Promise and Performance," *American Political Science Review* 79 (June 1985): 354.

14. Arthur H. Miller and Stephen A. Borelli, "Explaining Policy and Performance Orientations in the Electorate" (paper presented at American Political Science Association meeting, Chicago, 1987).

15. For example, G. Bingham Powell, *Contemporary Democracies* (Cambridge, Mass.: Harvard University Press, 1982), 208–12.

16. For example, see Dalton et al., *Electoral Change.*

17. Edward G. Carmines and James A. Stimson, "The Two Faces of Issue Voting," *American Political Science Review* 74 (March 1980): 78–91; Edward G. Carmines, Steven H. Renten, and James A. Stimson, "Events and Alignments," in *Controversies in Voting Behavior,* ed. Richard G. Niemi and Herbert F. Weisberg (Washington, D.C.: CQ Press, 1984), 545–60.

18. Paul Allen Beck, "Partisan Dealignment in the Postwar South," *American Political Science Review* 71 (June 1977): 480.

19. John Kenneth White, "The Rolling Republican Realignment" (paper presented at New York State Political Science Association meeting, New York, 1985).

20. Martin P. Wattenberg, *The Decline of American Political Parties* (Cambridge, Mass.: Harvard University Press, 1986).

21. Merrill Shanks and Warren E. Miller, "Policy Directions and Performance Evaluation" (paper presented at American Political Science Association meeting, New Orleans, 1985), 17–19.

22. Martin P. Wattenberg, "The Hollow Realignment" (paper presented at American Political Science Association meeting, New Orleans, 1985), 14.

23. Frank J. Sorauf and Paul Allen Beck, *Party Politics in America*, 6th ed. (Boston: Little, Brown, 1984), 481–95.

24. John F. Bibby, *Politics, Parties, and Elections in America* (Chicago: Nelson-Hall, 1987), 94–116.

25. Michael Margolis and Raymond E. Owen, "From Organization to Personalism," *Polity* 18 (Winter 1985): 313–28.

26. Joseph A. Schlesinger, "The New American Political Party," *American Political Science Review* 79 (December 1985): 1152–69.

27. John P. Frendreis, James L. Gibson, and Laura L. Vertz, "Local Party Organization in the 1984 Electorate" (paper presented at American Political Science Association Meeting, New Orleans, 1985).

28. John W. Kingdon, *Agendas, Alternatives, and Public Policies* (Boston: Little, Brown, 1984), 65–71.

29. Charles O. Jones, *An Introduction to the Study of Public Policy*, 3d ed. (Monterey, Calif.: Brooks/Cole, 1984), 115.

30. For a different analysis of operative values at work shaping elite decision making, see Dennis Coyle and Aaron Wildavsky, "Requisites of Radical Reform," *Journal of Policy Analysis and Management* 7 (Fall 1987): 1–16.

31. Jones, *Study of Public Policy*, 18.

CHAPTER 5

Policy Analysis and the Political Arena

When dealing with governmental institutions, the policy analyst confronts the structural manifestations of basic political values and the power of pluralism. The American people have had an enduring preference for government divided into many separate and largely uncoordinated units. The Founding Fathers' concern for the protection of liberty resulted in a tripartite division of the national government and a federal relationship between that government and the states. These structural arrangements have effectively limited the possibilities for efficient government through centralized direction. The divisive encroachments of social interests have fragmented the policy process further and have led scholars such as Lowi, Olson, and Huntington to voice concern about the direction of American democracy.[1] But experience with recent attempts to bring greater coherence into the policy process demonstrates that Americans continue to have little enthusiasm for coordinating or centralizing governmental institutions.

Coexisting, at times rather uncomfortably, with this distrust of centralized government has been a strong democratic spirit among Americans. Not only have Americans preferred fragmented governmental institutions, but they have insisted that these fragments be highly accessible to the people.[2] Furthermore, the larger the number of units and subunits of government, the greater the number of points where the citizen can "plug into the system," a fact not lost on the proliferating number of organized interests spawned by the nation's pluralistic society. This attachment to direct popular access was reinforced significantly by the Johnson administration's penchant for requiring citizen participation as a prerequisite to the implementation of federally funded programs at the local level. These requirements have often made life difficult for local policy makers and have at times raised questions about the viability of grass-roots participation.

The policy analyst intent on bringing to fruition the findings of a carefully designed and executed study may discover too late that the traditional political preferences of Americans often create impassable political roadblocks. At the national level and in many state and local jurisdictions, vested interests are adept at exploiting institutional fragmentation and use their direct access to obfuscate and delay even the most rationally defensible plans. The policy analyst must recognize the obstacles to orderly deliberation posed by the American political context and be prepared to work within the often emotional and chaotic conditions engendered by organized interests. Just as successful administrators within America's governmental bureaucracies have had to develop acute political skills, so the mature policy analyst needs to move beyond applying analytical techniques to an understanding of the political and normative environments in which findings and recommendations will be considered.

An Incremental Policy Process

Any policy analyst hoping to develop a more comprehensive sense of his or her position will inevitably confront the fact that the dominant theoretical framework for policy interpretation is itself limiting in perspective. To date, the guiding rationale or theory undergirding the policy process has been incrementalism. As perhaps its chief scholarly spokesman, Charles Lindblom has built a persuasive case for the rationality of step-by-step policy making. His position has been that incrementalism "is in fact a common method of policy formulation, and is, for complex problems, the principal reliance of administrators as well as of other policy analysts. And ... it will be superior to any other decision-making method available for complex problems in many circumstances."[3]

Pressed for time and information, policy makers cannot defer decisions, and it makes good sense for them to focus on specific incremental changes from current policy. Thus the cautious, politically wise administrator can retain a tentative stance and need not stray far from the known parameters of policy.

The administrator, in Lindblom's words (drawing on Herbert Simon), aims for "satisficing" decisions rather than the (rarely achievable) optimal resolution of a problem. He or she chooses an objective that could be viewed as a step in the right direction over an objective that calls for a definitive resolution of a problem or issue. From this position, an administrator can convey an image of moving toward solution and can at the same time retain the tactical flexibility to make revisions in response to feedback. There is no question that the incrementalist perspective meshes well with the bureaucratic conservatism and the fragmented nature of the policy process and that it creates a comfortable environment for the analytical technician. Careful study and slow, step-by-step development of policy are ideally suited to a process that features many centers of power.

Social Security Reform

A naïve disregard for the twin imperatives of incrementalism and fragmentation accounted in large part for the Reagan administration's early embarrassing defeat on the social security issue. As 1981 began, Congress had begun to confront the critical problem of ensuring the solvency of the Social Security System. Although the process was moving in the normal incremental, fragmented manner, some progress was being made. The chairman of the House Social Security subcommittee, Representative Jake Pickle, had fashioned a bill to deal with the problem and had obtained the tacit support of Representative Dan Rostenkowski, chairman of the parent Ways and Means Committee.

Coming from a Democratic chairman, the Pickle bill was at least a promising start toward bipartisan action. Moreover, it was faithful to Congress's strong preference for incrementalism. The retirement age would be raised from sixty-five to sixty-eight, and the proposed cuts of 16 percent in early retirement benefits were delayed until 1990. Saving social security was not to be accomplished by sudden, dramatic changes.

At this early point in the process, David Stockman, the new director of the Office of Management and Budget (OMB), entered the fray as the point man for the Reagan Administration. In 1981, Stockman's enthusiasm for the sweeping tax and spending cuts envisioned by the "Reagan Revolution" caused him to be unsympathetic to an incrementalist approach. For the Reagan program to work, drastic cuts in social security would have to be made quickly. To this end, Stockman drafted a proposal calling for a 25 percent reduction in early retirement benefits that would go into effect on 1 January 1982. There were other cost-cutting features in Stockman's draft, but the early retirement cuts proved to be what one White House aide termed "the lightning rod for opposition on Capitol Hill."[4]

Interest groups sprang into action when the Stockman proposal was placed before Congress. As a result of their activity, the political climate of social security reform had changed drastically by the time the Ways and Means Committee (whose chairman had originally supported the Pickle bill) held hearings on Stockman's suggestions. More than sixty groups testified against the early retirement cuts; not one testified in their favor. The final blow to these administration proposals came from the Republican-controlled Senate. On 20 May 1981, that body in effect killed social security reform for the time being by voting unanimously for a Republican-sponsored resolution declaring that "Congress shall not precipitously and unfairly penalize early retirees." Stockman, a former congressman himself, who as director of OMB had become a practitioner of rigorous analysis, later recognized that his zeal for radical change had contributed to the debacle. "Those of us who were pushing the policy," he acknowledged, "were totally negligent in looking at the politics."[5]

It is instructive that ultimately President Reagan had to move outside the normal congressional process to achieve a satisfactory resolution of the social security issue. He established a fifteen-member bipartisan National Commission on Social Security Reform to formulate a plan for maintaining the solvency of the Social Security System. Even this effort might have come to naught had it not been for the looming prospect that without further action all social security checks would be discontinued as of 3 July 1983.[6] With this crisis approaching, both Congress and the President found it prudent to accept the commission's recommendations for saving the Social Security System.

The Space Program

A major problem with incrementalism, in both theory and practice, is that it can provide neither the rationale nor the structure to support areas of public policy that require long-term planning and commitment. This shortsighted, self-interested characteristic of incrementalism seriously undercuts the efforts of policy analysts to provide coherence to the policy process and its goals, just as it undermined the viability of the Social Security System and the efforts to maintain it. America's manned space program has also illustrated the shortcomings of a policy process without either the institutional bases for long-term undertakings or a theoretical model able to provide coherent direction.

Examining the manned space program in 1975 Paul R. Schulman noted that it was one of a species of programs that "are enterprises distinguished by their demand for *comprehensive* rather than incremental decisions; synoptic rather than piecemeal outlooks and vision. These policies are characterized by an *indivisibility* in the political commitment and resources they require for success."[7] He argued that such programs cannot begin in small portions. They require "critical masses" of political and resource commitment at their inception, and at crucial points at their implementation.

In response to Sputnik and President John Kennedy's early enthusiasm, the manned space program obtained sufficient support to gain the funding necessary to land a person on the moon. But by the end of the 1960s, the centrifugal forces of policy fragmentation began to weaken America's commitment to the space program. Other priorities began to crowd onto the public agenda and claim their share of resources. At the same time, the lessening of support for the space program translated into lowered morale and competence there. The best people left to deal with new challenges, and those who remained did not retain the esprit de corps that had been generated for the lunar landing effort. Lowered morale made it increasingly difficult to maintain a high level of "hardware reliability and quality control," and insiders began to voice concern about the number of "glitches" occurring in projects.[8]

Programs requiring the level of commitment of the space program are not capable of a "steady state" existence. They are, Schulman argued, fundamentally unstable. To maintain support at a high level, administrators of these kinds of programs must articulate goals that will capture increasing resources. "The escalation of goals is a major requirement and a major dilemma of non-incremental policy."[9] For a time, the shuttle program instituted by President Nixon provided an important new goal for the space program. But it is clear that previous to the tragic *Challenger* disaster of January 1986, the space program was again striving for public commitment. This effort included sending civilians into space with the resultant publicity and—in the cases of Senator Jake Garn of the Senate Appropriations Committee and Congressman Bill Nelson of the House Science and Technology Committee—direct political support.

The public expectation of repeated successes placed pressure on the National Aeronautics and Space Administration (NASA) to continue to produce public events. Some of this was the result of attitudes encouraged by NASA's own public relations. Even the Rogers Commission Report, which was limited to investigating the cause of the *Challenger* accident, noted the "relentless pressure on NASA to increase the flight rate."[10] Situated in a fragmented policy process requiring an immense political effort to sustain continued heavy commitment, NASA was under constant pressure to perform at an exceptionally high level of technological complexity.

Schulman concluded his prescient piece by remarking on the inappropriateness of public policy models based on immediate concerns or self-interest for programs requiring exceptional levels of resources. He suggested that many of America's most serious problems required such programs.

Schulman's conclusions indicate that ongoing movement toward important policy goals may require the analyst to assume the role of advocate or at least to become allied with organizations capable of sustained political pressure.

Despite perceptive critiques of the incrementalist approach, there are no indications that it is about to be replaced or seriously challenged. The simple fact is that it fits exceptionally well with American political culture and institutions. It encourages gradual changes that are minimally threatening to organized interests. It facilitates the maintenance of policy fragmentation and citizen accessibility. And it provides stability and protection for the wary bureaucrat. The continued viability of incrementalist thought and practice ensures that definite limits on the boundaries of policy innovation and levels of programmatic support will remain obstacles to those hoping to wrestle with larger and more lasting goals.

A Fragmented Congress: The More Things Change, the More They Stay the Same

The American preference for weak, accessible government was fairly easy to translate into practice during the lengthy period from Jefferson's election as President in 1800 to Franklin D. Roosevelt's election to that office in 1932. Domestic and foreign policy problems during this period (with the exception of the Civil War and World War I) were relatively easy to manage and therefore required little governmental coordination. As a rule, the national government did very little during this period. The bulk of the responsibility of governing was carried out by numerous state and local governments that afforded a great deal of access to their constituents.

For its part, the national government replicated to a large extent the highly decentralized pattern set by state and local governments. The dominant branch of the national government was its most fragmented branch, the Congress. The politics of Congress was primarily patronage politics operating on an individual-to-individual or group-to-group basis.[11] Direct dealing with individual congressmen was the hallmark of the system. Coordinated national policy making was not its purpose.

The Great Depression of the 1930s, and more specifically the election of Franklin D. Roosevelt as President in 1932, brought two fundamental changes to the American political system. First, the balance of power and responsibility shifted decisively from state and local governments to the national government. Second, the focus of leadership *within* the national government shifted from Congress to the President. The President was now expected to provide leadership for the nation as a whole on a continuing basis. This expectation, backed by massive delegations of power to the executive branch by Congress and a burgeoning bureaucracy with its claims of administrative expertise, clearly placed the President in a preeminent position he had not enjoyed from 1800 to 1932.

Yet even in this new era of vastly expanded national government and presidential preeminence, the American people did not abandon their preference for fragmented government and their desire to have direct access to governmental units. Instead, they made the best adaptation possible under the vastly altered circumstances. The adaptation centered mainly on Congress.

While the President was expected to lead and coordinate, Congress was expected to play a representative role. State interests, district interests, and local interests had representation and access through their congressmen. In order to perform this function, Congress was expected to remain fragmented. Voters did not elect congressmen to coordinate national policy or lead the nation. They elected them, as they had in the past, primarily to represent their states and districts.[12]

Congress and the Subgovernment Phenomenon

The subgovernment phenomenon was and is an ingenious adaptation of the public's desire for direct access to the realities of the new era of big government. While not unknown before 1932, subgovernments proliferated and matured after that time. The committees and subcommittees in both houses of Congress are the central points of the subgovernments. They make recommendations to their parent bodies concerning the authorization and funding of government programs.[13] These recommendations are frequently, if not always, adopted by the House or Senate without major changes because rarely is either body in a position to challenge the expertise of the committees and especially the subcommittees.

A congressman typically seeks membership on committees or subcommittees that will give him power over programs that are of particular importance to his state or district. Many constituents with a strong interest in certain government programs belong to well-organized interest groups seeking direct access to the part of the government that oversees these programs. A link of mutual political advantage is formed between the congressman and the key interest groups in the district or state. The interest groups gain direct access, through the congressman and his committee, to the part of the decision-making process that directly concerns them. The congressman gains the political support of the interest groups, often in the form of campaign contributions for an upcoming election.

The congressman's committee or subcommittee and the concerned interest groups form two parts of a subgovernment. The third part is the agency in the executive branch that administers the programs of direct concern to the congressman's committee and the interest group. The agency is linked to the congressional committee or subcommittee because the authorizations and appropriations it needs usually depend on the committee or subcommittee recommendations. Interest groups that establish links with the pertinent committee or subcommittee of Congress also often serve as the clientele for agency programs and in the implementation of programs can provide a grass-roots political base for the agency. Thus a three-way linkup of mutual interest, sometimes depicted as a triangle, is formed between the committee or subcommittee, the affected groups, and the appropriate executive agency. Obviously, analysts employed by congressional subcommittees and interest groups have a clear sense of the policy directions in which their work should be pointed. But the subgovernment relationship works its will on agencies as well and encourages the "proper" orientation of analysts there also. It is quite possible, of course, for the participants in a policy issue to accept the general validity of analytical findings but disagree as to their importance. In such cases, the policy analyst has contributed to framing debate, even though the form of the final decision will rest with the policy makers themselves.

The triangular schema is in many ways a descriptively accurate depiction of the American policy process and in any event constitutes the core of that process. As used here, however, the idea of policy subgovernments also encompasses the broader idea of policy networks, which include the possibility of vertical, "picket fence" relationships among national, state, and local actors in particular policy areas. Within subgovernments, common professional, personal, and ideological associations not only influence policy preferences but also the beliefs that support them. Subgovernments are, then, more than good working relationships. They are the creators, preservers, and promulgators of particular values.

An excellent illustration of the subgovernment phenomenon can be found in the administration of the agricultural price-support program. The administration of this program is broken down according to major crops receiving federal price supports. Not surprisingly, a subgovernment has grown up around the program for each major crop in order to obtain the most favorable support possible for its producers.

In the House of Representatives, for example, the Cotton Subcommittee of the House Agriculture Committee takes special interest in federal supports for cotton. Congressmen from cotton-growing states typically seek membership on this subcommittee. The National Cotton Council, an interest group representing cotton growers, has strong links with congressmen on this subcommittee. Both the subcommittee and the interest group maintain strong ties with cotton specialists in the Agricultural Stabilization and Conservation Service (ASCS), the executive agency directly responsible for administering the agricultural price-support program.

Similar subgovernments revolve around support programs for oilseeds and rice, dairy and poultry products, livestock and grains, and tobacco. In the case of the latter, for example, a subgovernment consisting of the House Tobacco Subcommittee, the Tobacco Institute (an interest group), and tobacco specialists in the ASCS oversees federal supports for tobacco.[14] The interdependence of alliances is often further strengthened by the circulation of staff personnel among the constituent units of the subgovernment.

While these relationships are most salient at the national level, they exist as well at state and local levels, for any competent agency director will recognize the need to build a base of political support. Similarly, the student of policy analysis must develop awareness of the networks within which his or her proposals will be considered and formulate strategies that alleviate suspicion, uncertainty, and opposition whenever possible.

Congress and Constituent

The subgovernment phenomenon greatly increases direct access to contemporary "big government" largely on a group-to-group basis. Constituent services, in contrast, increase citizen access largely on an individual-to-individual basis. Like the subgovernments, constituent services have proliferated since 1932. Also, like subgovernments, they are sustained as much by public expectations as by congressmen's wishes. Both subgovernments and constituent services are devices by which congressmen bring an impersonal national government "down home" to the voters in the states and localities.

The nature of constituent services is illustrated by a communication sent by former Congressman Charles Wiggins to his constituents in the 39th Congressional District of California. "Need Help with a Federal Problem?" asks the headline. The communication goes on to advise the constituent: "If you are experiencing a problem with Social Security, educational assistance, Veterans Administration, Immigration, Internal Revenue Service, Postal Service, Environmental Protection Agency, Federal Energy Office, or any other federal agency, please contact me through this office."[15]

The enormous amount of time a congressman spends on constituent services is a further impediment to coordinated policy making by Congress. As one congressman observed: "One reason we are not able to formulate better national policy is because we have become the ombudsman and the last hope of individuals who are despairing of dealing with the federal bureaucracy." Yet Congress has consistently refused to act to improve direct citizen administrative access and thereby remove its members as political intermediaries.

In fragmenting its operations through subgovernments and constituent services, Congress has retained to a remarkable extent the highly particularized group-to-group and individual-to-individual politics that characterized its operations from 1800 to 1932. Congressmen believe, and the evidence clearly supports them, that they are acting in accord with what the public expects. A 1978 poll, for example, showed that while the public rated Congress *as a collective body* poorly (31 percent approval), they rated *their particular congressman* highly (62 percent approval).[16] Congressmen are well aware that their reelection depends much more on their performance as individual representatives than on the performance of Congress as a collective body.

The 1970s: Fragmentation Prospers in a Decade of Congressional Reform

During the 1970s, Congress instituted the most important procedural reforms since the House of Representatives stripped its Speaker of his far-reaching powers in 1910. The reformers of the 1970s did not set their sights on the fragmented structure of Congress. Instead, they sought primarily to democratize its internal procedures. By concentrating on the latter while deemphasizing the former, they increased the fragmentation that already existed.

Two important results of the reforms were (1) a dramatic decrease in the power of committee chairmen; and (2) an equally dramatic increase in the powers of subcommittees and their chairmen. Before the 1970s, it was virtually impossible to remove a committee chairman once the seniority rule had placed him on his perch. (The seniority rule mandates that the committee chairman be the majority party member with the longest continuous service on the committee.) During the 1970s, the Democrats, acting as the majority party in both the House and Senate, asserted their right to vote on, and if necessary remove, all committee chairmen. In 1975, House Democrats voted to remove three committee chairmen under the new rules. In 1973, House Democrats had enacted a "Subcommittee Bill of Rights" that sharply curtailed a committee chairman's power over the subcommittees under his jurisdiction.[17] For the most part, the powers lost by committee chairmen were not transferred to party leaders (who might have coordinated Congress) but to subcommittee chairmen and individual members. This further fragmented Congress and strengthened the subgovernment system.

The effect of increased subcommittee power was to narrow even further the policy-making incentives of congressmen and interest groups. When power rested at the committee level, and primarily with the chairman, there was an incentive to coordinate policy, at least at that level. The chairman could pressure the members of different subcommittees to modify and combine their particular preferences into a bill acceptable to him, or to the entire committee. Interest groups, working through a particular subcommittee, would likewise have to modify and confine their particular preferences with those of other interest groups in order to get a favorable bill.

The rise of subcommittee power in the 1970s drastically weakened these incentives. Because they could no longer be pressured to modify and combine their policy preferences, subcommittee chairmen and members were more likely to insist on their narrow policy preferences and to align their careers more closely with the small number of interest groups advocating them. Similarly, interest groups were encouraged to insist on their narrow preferences while concentrating exclusively on sympathetic subcommittees.[18] In the postreform environment, observes James Sundquist, "what begins as piecemeal consideration of problems in subcommittees of limited jurisdiction continues as piecemeal action through the legislative process."[19] The effects of this process on efforts to coordinate such areas as environmental policy or health policy are, of course, disastrous. At the same time, the increased fragmentation further encourages the advocacy role of the policy analyst. Whether employed by an interest group or subcommittee, analysts inevitably find themselves moving in narrower political channels. In this environment, concerns about the overall effects of a policy position on health care may be more easily subordinated to supporting more intensely the interests of hospitals or the medical profession.

The 1970s: What Congress Did Not Do
To say that Congress deemphasized coordination of its fragmented procedures in the 1970s is not to say it gave the matter no attention at all. But with the notable exception of changes in its budgeting procedures, the efforts given to coordinating its internal procedures came to very little. In these attempts to make the legislative process more coherent and rational, policy analysts supporting change were badly battered by the political power of organized interests that wished to maintain the free rein given to issue advocacy.

Both houses established special committees to make recommendations about how to improve the coordination of internal procedures. The Bolling Committee, established by the House of Representatives for this purpose, recommended reducing the number of committees and subcommittees, and altering their jurisdiction. The Bolling proposals encountered determined resistance, much of it in the form of "reverse lobbying."

Normal lobbying occurs when an interest group exerts pressure on congressmen or their staffs. In the case of the Bolling proposals, congressmen and their staffs exerted pressure on the interest groups to lobby against the proposals. Congressmen, their staffs, and affected interest groups all saw a danger to longstanding links of mutual influence within subgovernments. As a result, the Bolling proposals were rejected or greatly weakened.[20] For example, in moves to appease key labor unions and their congressional supporters, the Education and Labor Committee was kept intact, the Post Office and Civil Service Committee was retained, and the Merchant Marine and Fisheries Committee was strengthened rather than weakened. The continued dominance of these centers of power also has unhappy ramifications for the concept of coherent administrative policy in the executive branch. Attempts to rationalize agency structure through reorganization face the same kinds of pressures as the Bolling proposals from committees and interests that see their areas of jurisdiction and access threatened by changes in agency structure and personnel. Finally, the *intensity* of the opposition aroused to proposals for greater legislative and administrative coordination is an added impediment to comprehensive analysis and planning within the subgovernment network.

A clear contrast emerges between the enthusiasm and determination with which Congress democratized and fragmented its internal procedures and the lack of enthusiasm when efforts to consolidate and coordinate those procedures were under way. Lack of enthusiasm has likewise been the common response to proposals, often made by experts outside Congress, to strengthen the party leadership apparatus in Congress while weakening the power of special interest groups. Such proposals are usually championed as legitimate political devices to centralize and coordinate the internal workings of Congress.

Everett Carll Ladd, for example, has proposed that federal funding should be extended to congressional election campaigns. These federal funds would be administered by party committees in each house. The funds, therefore, would go only to central party organs, not directly to candidates. Candidates could raise funds from special interest groups, but the amounts that such groups could give would be very strictly limited.[21] The purpose of Ladd's proposal is clearly to strengthen the two broad-based national parties as centralizing and coordinating forces in Congress while weakening the power of narrowly-based special interest groups that fragment that body. Congressmen, interest groups, and the public at large all tend to regard strong parties in Congress as an impediment to direct relations between congressmen and their constituents. Therefore, nothing was done in the 1970s to strengthen parties at the expense of interest groups.

On the contrary, in 1973 Congress took action that had the opposite effect. Prompted by business and labor groups, it amended the U.S. Code to allow corporations with government contracts (which included most large corporations) to form political action committees (PACs) that would enable these corporations to contribute money to congressional campaigns. Corporate motives in supporting this change were obvious. The AFL-CIO, on the other hand, was motivated by the fear that its political action committee (Committee on Political Education) might soon be included under the statutory ban on PACs, since it had a number of manpower training contracts with the federal government.[22]

This congressional action was one of several factors that contributed to the explosion in the number of PACs in the 1970s and 1980s. The total number of PACs registered with the Federal Election Commission rose from 608 in 1974, to 3371 at the end of 1982.[23] By strengthening PACs, Congress further contributed to its own fragmentation as a legislative body, because PACs concentrate on narrow issues and work with congressmen individually. In this respect, their advocacy of self-interested or ideologically rigid values has seriously hindered the development of a general normative framework for coherent policy. PACs have no interest whatsoever in coordinating policy from a national perspective as do political parties. At the fund-raising and governing stages of politics, PACs are the institutional competitors of political parties.[24] The sizable boost Congress gave to the former, therefore, served to weaken further the coordinating powers of the latter.

The activities of the "reform decade" of the 1970s did little to change Congress's historical tradition as a highly fragmented body. Indeed, the end of the decade found Congress more divided than ever before. The reasons for this outcome are not difficult to discern. The public expectations of congressmen (that they be first and foremost representatives of their states and districts) did not change during the decade. Therefore, their basic incentives did not change. Reforms that did not conflict with these basic incentives (democratizing congressional procedures) fared very well. Those that did (consolidating and coordinating the committee structures, strengthening the role of parties) had little or no success.

The Presidency: The Problem of Fragmentation in the "Leadership Branch"

After 1932, the public's expectations of the President (unlike those of Congress) underwent a dramatic change. Before 1932, Presidents were expected to assert themselves as national leaders only on an intermittent basis. The Great Depression and World War II changed that modest expectation permanently. The President was now expected to exercise strong national leadership on a continuing basis. The President's job was to chart the course for the nation and coordinate national policies in order to follow that course. Yet even in the "leadership branch" the problem of fragmentation, while not nearly as severe as in Congress, presents serious problems for coordinating public policy.

Presidential Nominations: Reforms Bring Fragmentation

During the late 1960s and 1970s, the Democratic party enacted historic changes in the way it nominated its presidential candidates. There are interesting parallels between those reforms and the procedural reforms enacted by Congress in roughly the same period. Both sought, with great success, to democratize procedures. In doing this, both radically reduced the powers of established leaders who had helped to coordinate operations. Yet neither provided new leadership centers to assume coordinating responsibilities. The congressional reforms weakened committee chairmen. The Democratic party reforms weakened traditional party leaders outside Congress. In both cases, special-interest groups filled a large part of the power vacuum. And in both cases, changes initiated by Democrats led to similar changes by Republicans.

The decline of traditional party leaders in the Democratic and Republican parties led to the decline of an important coordinating function they had performed—coalition building and the construction of minimal normative consensus. Three decades ago, party leaders had the power to pressure special-interest groups to modify their demands as the price of becoming part of a national party coalition that could win the Presidency. Using this power, party leaders could act as a buffer between presidential candidates and special-interest groups, especially during the presidential nomination phase. In the postreform era, party leaders are much more limited in their power to modify the demands of special-interest groups on the party or on presidential candidates.

Candidates for the presidential nomination are more than ever dependent on the direct support and approval of special-interest groups.[25] Public postures they must take in behalf of these groups during the quest for party nomination or renomination may render them less able, if nominated and elected, effectively to coordinate public policies for the nation. In 1984, Walter Mondale's highly visible strategy of seeking advance endorsements for his party's nomination from labor groups, women's groups, and minority groups led to the damaging public perception that he had been compromised as a national leader by this strategy.

Ronald Reagan was far more successful for a number of reasons. As the long-time leader of the insurgent conservative movement against established party leaders in the Republican party, he had probably internalized the programmatic agenda of conservative interest groups more than Mondale had internalized the agendas of corresponding liberal groups. Thus Reagan projected a stronger image of genuine conviction to the voters. Moreover, in 1980, the general public was moving in Reagan's conservative direction more than in the Democratic party's liberal direction.

Yet Reagan, like Mondale, was nominated in the postreform environment of strong special-interest groups and weak party leaders. Acting in accord with key items on the agenda of conservative interest groups, President Reagan successfully urged Congress to enact an extremely ambitious military buildup and a package of large tax cuts. In these and other important initiatives, the Reagan people drew heavily on the recommendations of conservative policy analysts from such think tanks as the Heritage Foundation, the Hoover and Claremont Institutes, and the American Enterprise Institute. In fact, since the Nixon administration, a fairly extensive network of conservative academic and nonacademic thinkers interested in policy questions had developed. This network meshed easily with the Reagan administration people and their goals.

Moderate Republican leaders, who were less closely identified with these groups, were concerned from the outset about lack of policy coordination in the Reagan program. How could huge tax cuts finance a huge military buildup? What about the traditional Republican adage that large deficits arise when taxing and spending policies are not coordinated?[26] By 1986, the concerns of the moderates had proved to be prophetic. Despite the fact that Reagan was one of the politically strongest and most popular Presidents since FDR, his unbalanced fiscal policies raised serious questions about the ability of any President nominated largely through the influence of interest groups to coordinate national public policies once elected. Unlike other postwar Republican Presidents, Reagan at least had a majority in the Senate during the first six years of his administration. But the loss of the Senate in 1986 opened the door wider to interest-group politics, and the President's ability to lead dissipated rapidly.

The Endless Struggle for Executive Coordination
The executive branch of the national government is composed of 13 separate departments and 120 special agencies that together employ approximately 3 million civilian employees.[27] Although the President is referred to as the "chief executive" of this vast bureaucracy, his power to coordinate its activities is extremely limited. Of the 3 million civilian bureaucrats, only about 2700 can be hired or removed at the President's pleasure. The rest are career civil servants, who are hired and fired according to merit principles determined by the Office of Personnel Management.[28]

The primary loyalty of career civil servants is to their agency (which is their permanent working environment and economic support system), rather than to the President (who is to them a temporary political phenomenon). At the top of the career bureaucracy are approximately 4000 men and women with considerable policy-making powers.[29] Over the years, many of them have established durable relationships with pertinent interest groups and congressmen on key committees and subcommittees. In so doing, they have become one of the links in the subgovernment triangles.

Standing between the President and the career bureaucracy are cabinet and subcabinet officials who serve at the President's pleasure and are supposed to manage their departments and agencies according to the President's priorities. In theory, these officials are "the President's people"; in practice, they are more often "people in the middle." They are subject to pressures from the President and his White House staff and at the same time expected to respond sympathetically to more narrow agency interests articulated by career administrators who may be supported by key congressmen and clientele interest groups. Although the balancing acts required of cabinet and subcabinet officials at the national level are most salient to the media and general public, the political and administrative cross-pressures they face are common to politically appointed administrators at any level of the American system.

Under these circumstances, it is not surprising that these officials have divided loyalties and often displease chief executives who appoint them. The phenomenon of divided loyalties helps explain why repeated attempts by Presidents to coordinate executive policy through their cabinets (often called "cabinet government") have typically ended in failure. It can explain also why agencies presented with proposals that appear eminently rational in their approach to problems fail to act forthrightly or coherently toward implementation of these ideas. These conditions can put severe strains on the integrity of the policy analyst, who, caught in the cross-pressures of bureaucratic politics, may face subtle and not so subtle pressures to shade and skew findings to fit political needs or expectations. On the other hand, there will be many instances when an analyst may justifiably insist that his or her agency's position requires that a particular emphasis be given to the results of a study.

Strategies for Fighting Bureaucratic Fragmentation

All postwar Presidents have expressed frustration at their inability to coordinate policy through the executive branch. Major expansions of the federal bureaucracy in the domestic area have resulted from the initiatives of liberal Democratic Presidents primarily interested in establishing substantive programs reaching particular segments of the population. Republican Presidents, on the other hand, have often been ideologically unsympathetic to these programs and in any event have been uniformly more interested in achieving administrative efficiency in their implementation. Consequently, recent Republican Presidents have found the political power and fragmentation of the bureaucracy particularly frustrating[30] and have worked at making it more responsive to their direction. Both Nixon and Reagan provide instructive examples of the possibilities that exist for moving toward a more coherent and presidentially responsive bureaucracy.

What is of particular note with regard to the management efforts of

Nixon and Reagan is their recognition of the political forces at work in their administrations and in the intergovernmental implementation of programs. In contrast, President Johnson largely overlooked these political forces in seeking increased control through the Planning, Program, Budgeting System (PPBS) approach. In 1965 he ordered it instituted throughout the government. PPBS was no doubt attractive to the President because it necessitated the definition of policy goals at the highest levels and then moved resources in line with these goals. In this emphasis on policy outputs, PPBS directly challenged the traditional line-item approach to budgeting, which had become a staple of agency power and incremental policy making. Furthermore, PPBS was no respecter of organizational boundaries or interests. As B. Guy Peters puts it: "In short, PPBS was a dagger pointed toward the central role of the agency in policymaking in the federal government, and as such it could not really have been expected to be successful...."[31]

With its emphasis on program outputs, PPBS may in retrospect stand as a turning point in the primary focus of public budgeting theory. As a technique for increased executive control of the bureaucracy, however, it foundered on the opposition of an entire system built around fragmented power. Perhaps somewhat wiser because of President Johnson's experience, Presidents Nixon and Reagan approached the problem of control from routes that did not so blatantly challenge vested power interests. They had concluded that effective program administration required something more politically tangible and persuasive than analytical prowess.

Soon after taking office, Richard Nixon gave up hope of coordinating the executive bureaucracy through his cabinet members. Instead, he used his White House staff as a "counterbureaucracy." Unlike cabinet members, White House staffers have a working environment incontestably dominated by the President, and therefore they must manifest an undivided loyalty to him. Nixon directed his White House staff to oversee an increasing number of bureaucratic activities. Final clearance for bureaucratic initiative was largely transferred from cabinet members to White House staffers.

The "counterbureaucracy" strategy backfired in an ironic way. In order to exert control over bureaucratic policy making, Nixon's White House staffers had to become increasingly involved in administrative details. As they became deeply involved in details, they had less time to oversee important areas of bureaucratic policy making. Career bureaucrats were increasingly able to make important policy decisions without clearance from a harried White House staff.[32] As a result, policy advocacy moved by default from the White House to the less coordinated domain of agency turf.

In his second term, Nixon turned to a different strategy of asserting presidential control. He decided to elevate several of his most loyal and effective cabinet members to the status of supersecretaries overseeing clusters of government departments in broad functional areas. The role and size of the White House staff were to be largely curtailed in Nixon's second term, but three top-level White House staffers were assigned to help the supersecretaries "integrate and unify policies and operations throughout the executive branch."[33] The second-term strategy of presidential control was launched just at the time the Watergate scandals crashed down on the Nixon administration. The scandals weakened and finally destroyed the administration and, along with it, the second-term effort at presidential control of the bureaucracy.

Ronald Reagan's strategy for asserting presidential control of the bureaucracy was less complex but at the same time more effective than Richard Nixon's. Reagan concentrated mainly on the appointments process. Nixon learned, only after some costly mistakes, that appointing administration loyalists to subcabinet posts was as important as appointing them to cabinet posts. The Reagan administration understood and acted on this axiom from the beginning. Moreover, more than any previous administration, it also emphasized the importance of placing Reagan loyalists in appointive positions *below* the subcabinet level. Thus the administration was able to penetrate more deeply into the executive bureaucracy than any before it and to establish a level of ideological consistency unmatched by any previous administration.

Like Nixon, Reagan understood the importance of loyalty of appointees to the administration. The Reagan administration, however, was more thorough in the measures it took to ensure that loyalty. In filling some 430 appointive posts, three or four finalists were sought for each post. Interviews conducted by Reagan staffers with eight to ten people who knew each candidate were instrumental in the decision process. Appointees were expected to be loyal to Ronald Reagan and to the conservative movement. Since Reagan had led that movement within the Republican party since 1968, the two loyalties were mutually reinforcing.

To maintain a high level of loyalty among appointees, the administration, to an unusual degree, utilized an orientation process separate from the bureaucracy. During the transition period, cabinet members learned about their departments from conservative task forces rather than from career personnel in their agencies. Several breakfast meetings with large numbers of subcabinet appointees were held each year featuring President Reagan, Vice-

President Bush, and high-level White House or cabinet officials as speakers.[34]

If, as the studies examined in chapter 2 suggest, policy makers in uncertain situations tend to act from their political convictions, then it seems likely that the Reagan approach to personnel recruitment had the effect of creating a reasonably homogeneous normative framework for the consideration of policy recommendations.

After the first term in office, the Reagan administration had proven more successful than its predecessors in moving the executive bureaucracy in directions desired by its President. Nevertheless, there were severe limits even on Reagan's relatively successful strategy. One of the most important of these was that Congress, as well as the President, has much to say about how the executive bureaucracy functions. Thus Congress was able to blunt or block many initiatives of Reagan appointees when they were perceived as too zealous in their attempts to redefine or ignore the clear intent of laws specifying the objectives of executive agencies such as the Environmental Protection Agency. Still, given the broad initiatives undertaken against many bureaucratic interests, the administration was relatively free from internal conflicts. Clearly, the strong ideological stance of the White House encouraged analysis that fit their views and muted that which did not.

At the same time, congressmen continued to have an interest in keeping the executive branch as fragmented as possible so as to increase their direct access and that of their group allies. The Reagan administration demonstrated imagination and political effectiveness in attacking subgovernment strongholds through the use of block grants. Unlike categorical grants, which are directed at specific programs and administered by bureaucratic specialists who develop close ties with clientele and congressional subcommittees, block grants eliminate many of the specific requirements that necessitate bureaucratic monitoring. They make funds available for general purposes whose details are determined by state and local governments. The block-grant approach generated considerable political support from state and local officials. This backing counteracted the power of the subgovernments, which also found their effective agency component under heavy budgetary pressures from the Reagan administration's attacks on domestic spending. The early results of the Reagan efforts to repackage domestic spending suggest that this approach weakened administrative resistance to presidential directives and that it may have engendered new political networks, perhaps resembling the subgovernment model, at state and local levels.

The Crisis of Fragmented Government: The Loss of Fiscal Discipline

The American preference for the fragmented forms of the governmental system has made policy coordination through the budgetary process particularly difficult to achieve. The costs of fragmented government were tolerable under the conditions of high prosperity and rapid economic growth that characterized the 1945-65 period. Since that time, however, the economy has become less prosperous. Slowly but surely, awareness has grown that fragmented government cannot set spending priorities or control spending in an increasingly difficult economic environment. Efforts to achieve fiscal discipline by coordinating governmental machinery began in the 1970s and continued into the 1990s. Most noticeably at the federal level, these efforts have not succeeded, due in part to the fact that in many instances they have threatened the very existence of particular subgovernments. Their failure has ushered in the danger of a complete breakdown of fiscal discipline.

The Rise and Fall of the Budget Process in Congress

In 1974, Congress established budget committees for each of its two houses. These committees were charged with establishing spending limits for each of the seventeen broad categories in the federal budget.[35] The two committees were expected to bring fiscal coordination and discipline to the numerous other committees and subcommittees that had failed to accomplish either goal in the past.

Although the creation of the budget committees was the most significant step Congress took toward coordinating its procedures in the 1970s, the inherent limits of the process working effectively on its own were severe. A floor vote of either house could overturn the recommendations of its budget committee in favor of the recommendations of its older fragmented and logrolling committees. From the outset, it seemed clear that only with the help of strong presidential leadership would the budget committees win decisive victories for budgetary coordination and fiscal discipline.

In 1981, President Reagan provided such leadership and exercised it largely through the two budget committees. By presenting his proposals for an unprecedented $40 billion in spending cuts to the budget committees, and insisting on quick, decisive action on their recommendations, the President forced Congress to vote on broad rather than narrow categories of spending. The older logrolling committees and subcommittees simply did not have time to break these broad categories down into their program-size components and to rally affected interest groups to restore funds for their programs.[36]

Unfortunately, the triumph of the presidentially activated budget committees did not last after 1981. Despite his budget cuts, the President's own budget was badly out of balance and poorly coordinated, partly because of massive defense increases that were to be financed in the face of huge tax cuts. The budget committee leaders were willing to compromise on a number of their own program priorities in order to restore fiscal discipline through the new budget process, but the President was considerably less willing to do so. When the budget committee chairmen and other congressional leaders suggested a bipartisan compromise, which included raising taxes and lowering the growth rate of military spending, in order to lower federal deficits, the President abandoned the two committee leaders and the new budget process.

By the summer of 1983, a number of press reports stated that the President "would be perfectly happy to see the budget process fall on its face" rather than alter his priorities on military spending and taxes. Secretary of Defense Caspar Weinberger reported that the President had referred to the new budget process as a "Rube Goldberg machine."[37] Left on their own, the budget committees could win no more decisive victories for fiscal discipline and budgetary coordination. Annual federal deficits ballooned from $60 billion to more than $200 billion by 1986.

The Gramm-Rudman Proposal: An Attempt at
Fiscal Coordination by Shotgun

The budget process had been the main hope of congressmen who wished to discipline and coordinate fiscal policy within the Congress. This proved to be impossible without strong presidential leadership that could wrench Congress out of its normal pattern of fragmented decision making and forge a coordinated policy between the two houses of Congress and the President. When President Reagan proved unwilling to lead a sustained bipartisan effort to achieve these objectives, an atmosphere of desperation began to grow in Congress. In this context, the Gramm-Rudman proposal passed both houses of Congress and was signed into law by President Reagan at the end of 1985. The proposal was intended to force the President and Congress to make the compromises necessary to coordinate and discipline fiscal policy and was a kind of self-imposed "shotgun marriage" between the President and Congress. Significantly, Gramm-Rudman became law without going through normal congressional procedures and thus avoided the fragmentation and delay that it would have faced in public hearings, committee debate, and debate on the House floor. Although not formalized, the short-circuiting of congressional procedures became a common approach toward dealing with major budget, tax, and social security legislation under the Reagan administration.

The Gramm-Rudman bill, passed in December 1985, set a strict timetable for eliminating federal deficits by 1991. The 1986 deficit target was set at $171.9 billion; the 1987 target would drop to $144 billion. In each successive year, deficits would be reduced by $36 billion until they were eliminated in 1991.[38] The "shotgun" feature of the law was straightforward. If the President and Congress could not reach an agreement in any given year about how the deficit should be reduced, deficit reduction would proceed according to an automatic formula that would largely displace both the President and Congress from the process.

The formula designed for the 1987 budget illustrated how the process would work. By 3 February, the President had to recommend, and by 15 June, Congress had to complete deficit reduction legislation. If the predicted deficit exceeded that year's $144 billion target by more than $10 billion, the General Accounting Office was to formulate across-the-board spending reductions. Approximately one-half of these were to come from defense spending, and one-half from domestic spending. Two large spending areas (social security and interest on the national debt) and some smaller social spending programs helping mainly the poor were exempted in advance by Gramm-Rudman. Without question, Gramm-Rudman was an admission by congressmen of their inability to overcome the entrenched fragmentation they had encouraged. Its passage indicated that the inability of the federal government to coordinate fiscal policy (the most basic policy of all) had reached a crisis stage in the minds of the nation's highest elected officials.

In another sense, Gramm-Rudman may have been one of the finer moments for policy analysis in the national policy process. The measure was based on a thoughtful judgment as to the dangers posed by continued fiscal irresponsibility. Its approach toward fiscal discipline combined analytical understanding of the problem, a fine sense of timing, and a knowledgeable anticipation of the realities of the congressional process. Thus the analytical findings suggesting an effective approach were tempered by reasonable political compromises (on social security, for example) and by providing Congress and the President with an opportunity to reach agreement on their own. But the bottom line on the legislation was that it moved national budget policy in a rational, deliberate manner toward greater control and responsibility. Imposition of the remaining automatic cuts would drastically reduce, or eliminate, many popular domestic programs cherished by Congress and many defense programs cherished by the President. The automatic formula would largely replace both the President's priorities and those of Congress. The supporters of Gramm-Rudman reasoned that the prospect of invoking the automatic formula would be so repugnant to the President and Congress that they would finally reach their own deficit-reduction compromises.

Gramm-Rudman was launched in a sea of doubt concerning how long the shotgun marriage between the two branches could last, or if it would work at all. The core problem remained one of coordination. As various groups of Americans actually began to experience the effects of automatic slashes in domestic programs, they might successfully lobby Congress to add those programs to the original list of exemptions. Similarly, as slashes in defense spending programs were made, the President might insist on their exemption in the name of national security.

Gramm-Rudman, while very dramatic, was only a law. It neither changed basic political relationships nor modified Americans' normative attachment to divided government. Thus it could be easily weakened or rendered ineffectual. In fact, the law existed under a constitutional cloud from its inception. Twelve House members who had opposed its passage immediately challenged its constitutionality in the federal courts. In July 1986, the Supreme Court declared unconstitutional the automatic spending-cut provisions of Gramm-Rudman.[39] Congress had provided that these cuts were to be made by the comptroller general, who heads the General Accounting Office, an agency responsible to Congress. The Court concluded that this violated the constitutional clause requiring that the President see that the laws are faithfully executed. It reasoned that placing the comptroller general in charge of automatic budget cuts had the effect of making the Congress an executor of the law.

The merits of the decision are less important here than its significance as another ramification of the policy process. In this instance, the courts, yet another part of the fragmented scheme of American government, had been called on to weaken, if not destroy, a crisis-induced agreement reached grudgingly by the deadlocked elected branches of the national government. Gramm-Rudman was not eliminated by the Supreme Court decision, but its effectiveness became very questionable. In particular, who would or could impose automatic budget cuts in the likely event of a presidential-congressional impasse remained undetermined. Congress resolved the question in 1987 by passing legislation (P.L. 100-199) giving this power under strict guidelines to the Office of Management and Budget, an executive agency.

Fiscal Discipline by Constitutional Mandate
During the 1970s and 1980s, a movement outside Congress to require the federal government to balance its budget (and thereby eliminate its deficits every fiscal year) made substantial progress. The device to achieve this end would not be an ordinary law passed by Congress but a change in the U.S. Constitution. By 1985, thirty-two states had issued a call for a new constitutional convention, only two states short of the thirty-four needed to call such an extraordinary body. Theoretically, such a convention could rewrite the entire Constitution. Proponents, however, claimed that it would limit itself to the "balanced budget" amendment.

But even if such an amendment were passed, it would face problems similar to those of Gramm-Rudman. After the amendment has been ratified, how can it be enforced on a fragmented national government? The American Constitution creates not one but three elected national governments: the House of Representatives, the Senate, the Presidency. The Constitution establishes the independence of all three, and provides no mechanisms for coordinating them. In this respect, an amendment that does not reconstitute basic political relationships can hardly be more effective than a statute. Proponents of a constitutional mandate tend to oppose an activist Supreme Court. Yet the Court, in its traditional role as the final arbiter of the Constitution, might become the final arbiter of the federal budget. More likely, a four-way struggle among the three elected branches and the federal courts headed by the Supreme Court would ensue. The result could be even more fragmentation and policy instability than now exist.

Policy Analysis and Political Uncertainty
The policy process can be unnerving to the uninitiated. The policy analyst is trained in the application of rational methods to problems, and his or her conclusions often possess an aura of certainty. There may not be one best way of dealing with a problem, but usually analysis will suggest two or three clearly preferable alternatives. Unfortunately for the analyst, who may have devoted considerable time and effort to a problem, the policy process can easily proceed to unravel the most tightly reasoned positions, or even

worse, may simply ignore them. Constituent interests, agency rivalries, congressional infighting, or external political considerations are but a few of the factors that have priority over rationally based findings and recommendations. The less established the context and relationships in which an issue is to be decided, the more unpredictable will be the factors that will impinge on the recommendations made.

It should be emphasized that the student of public policy should expect to find at state and local levels of politics relationships similar to those at the national level. Although political structural configurations will vary, the need for administrators to establish political bases, the power of the legislative committees, and the existence of organized interests are common to all levels of American government and to almost all areas of public policy. Where subgovernments have established themselves over time, policy is often reasonably predictable and coherent. In these situations, the advantages of close working relationships, a common sense of mission, and experience can contribute significantly to the effective implementation of routine policy. When this routine is threatened by changes in policy direction or by competing subsystems, established subgovernments have demonstrated time and time again that they can be serious obstacles to the coordinated implementation of public policy and the acceptance of the ideas of policy analysts.

The policy process seems to function most rationally and effectively in the face of crisis. When confronted with impending disaster, or in times of serious difficulties, the actors in the policy process appear able to rouse themselves from the bonds of meandering incrementalism sufficiently to formulate solutions. But their success in taking bold action often depends on their willingness to bypass the fragmented policy process. Often these situations provide important opportunities for the suggestions of policy analysts. Once the issue is resolved, however, incremental change in diverse directions again becomes dominant, and even the long-term policy commitments obtained can become vulnerable to forces moved by short-term self-interest.

Notes

1. Theodore J. Lowi, *The End of Liberalism: The Second Republic of the United States,* 2d ed. (New York: Norton, 1979); Mancur Olson, *The Rise and Decline of Nations* (New Haven: Yale University Press, 1982); and Samuel P.

Huntington, *American Politics* (Cambridge, Mass.: Harvard University Press, 1981).

2. Bert A. Rockman, *The Leadership Question* (New York: Praeger, 1985), 40–41.

3. Charles E. Lindblom, "The Science of 'Muddling Through,'" *Public Administration Review* 19 (Spring 1959): 88.

4. Paul Light, *Artful Work* (New York: Random House, 1985), 117, 121.

5. Ibid., 122–25.

6. Ibid., 137.

7. Paul R. Schulman, "Nonincremental Policy Making: Notes toward an Alternative Paradigm," *American Political Science Review* 69 (December 1975): 1355.

8. Ibid., 1364.

9. Ibid., 1366.

10. "Rogers Commission Recommendations," *Congressional Quarterly Weekly Report* 44 (14 June 1986): 1326.

11. Theodore J. Lowi, *The Personal President* (Ithaca, N.Y.: Cornell University Press, 1985), 25.

12. James L. Sundquist, *The Decline and Resurgence of Congress* (Washington, D.C.: Brookings Institution, 1981), 441.

13. Randall B. Ripley and Grace A. Franklin, *Congress, The Bureaucracy and Public Policy*, rev. ed. (Homewood, Ill.: Dorsey Press, 1980), 96.

14. Ibid., 97.

15. Cited in Morris P. Fiorina, *Congress* (New Haven: Yale University Press, 1977), 49.

16. Sundquist, *Decline and Resurgence*, 446.

17. Lawrence C. Dodd and Bruce I. Oppenheimer, "The House in Transition: Change and Consolidation," in *Congress Reconsidered*, ed. Lawrence C. Dodd and Bruce I. Oppenheimer, 2d ed. (Washington, D.C.: CQ Press, 1981), 41, 44.

18. Ibid., 45–46.

19. Sundquist, *Decline and Resurgence*, 432.

20. Roger H. Davidson, "Two Avenues of Change: House and Senate Committee Reorganization," in Dodd and Oppenheimer, *Congress Reconsidered*, 116–17.

21. Everett Carll Ladd, "How to Tame the Special-Interest Groups," *Fortune*, 20 October 1980, 66–80.

22. Mark Green, "Political PAC-Man," *New Republic*, 13 December 1982, 24.

23. David Adamany, "Political Parties in the 1980s," in *Money and Politics in the United States,* ed. Michael J. Malbin (Washington, D.C.: American Enterprise Institute, 1984), 102.

24. Ibid., 101.

25. Edward N. Kearny, "Presidential Nominations and Representative Democracy: Proposals for Change," *Presidential Studies Quarterly,* Summer 1984, 350–51.

26. Herbert Stein, *Presidential Economics* (New York: Simon and Schuster, 1984), 272–73.

27. Robert E. DiClerico, *The American President,* 2d ed. (Englewood Cliffs, N.J.: Prentice-Hall, 1983), 111.

28. Ibid., 114.

29. Ibid.

30. Ibid., 115.

31. B. Guy Peters, *American Public Policy,* 2d ed. (Chatham, N.J.: Chatham House, 1986), 125.

32. Richard P. Nathan, *The Administrative Presidency* (New York: Wiley, 1983), 40–41.

33. Ibid., 51–52.

34. Ibid., 74–76.

35. DiClerico, *American President,* 84.

36. Harold Wolman and Fred Teitelbaum, "Interest Groups and the Reagan Presidency," in *The Reagan Presidency and the Governing of America,* ed. Lester M. Salamon and Michael S. Lund (Washington, D.C.: Urban Institute Press, 1984), 307.

37. Dick Kirschten, "If It Needs Fixin'," *National Journal,* 9 July 1983, 1460.

38. *Washington Post National Weekly Edition,* 23 December 1985, 12.

39. *Bowsher* v. *Synar,* 478 U.S. 714.

CHAPTER 6

Policy Analysis in the Judicial Process

Policy disarray in the elected branches of government has contributed significantly toward involving the nation's courts more actively in the making of policy. Relatively insulated from political pressures, courts remain capable of providing reasonably definitive, authoritative responses to the questions brought before them. Thus there has been a tendency by elected policy makers and the public to defer difficult and controversial issues to what seem to be the impartial, rational processes of judicial procedure. The courts in turn have abetted this movement by easing the requirements for standing to sue and by adopting a more activist view of the judicial role. In trying to manage complex social problems, judges have often turned to various forms of social and scientific analysis to complement the formalities of judicial procedure. The courts have never really been comfortable with such approaches, however, and in their grappling with social problems they have illustrated the policy limitations of the legal process.

The Judicial Process

Since the days of the early common-law courts of England, Anglo-American judges have served to integrate changing social norms into the law of the land. The framework for this activity has been the common law and the dynamic of the adversary process. In the adversary process, the parties to a case present to the court not only interpretations as to the facts involved but also their views as to the appropriate rule of law governing the case. In suggesting the proper rule of law, attorneys to a case where there is no statute involved utilize previous judicial decisions, or legal precedents, that support their positions. They in effect ask a judge or a panel of judges to legitimize or penalize a particular form of conduct and thus render it legally acceptable or unacceptable. Judges, in an incremental fashion, draw on earlier judicial positions to determine which view of legitimacy will prevail in the case before them. This decision in turn becomes part of the collection of judicial precedents on which later litigants and judges will rely. As social norms change, new legal arguments are brought before the courts. Judges will act to incorporate some of these into legal rules over a period of time and a succession of cases.

Although the proliferation of statute law has rendered common law, or judge-made law, less influential in many areas, the courts have retained their roles as arbiters of competing social norms. No statute can encompass every circumstance to which it might be applied, and statutory language, no matter how carefully chosen, will require some elaboration by the courts. But today, precision in statutory language is the rare exception. It is far more common practice for state and national legislators to skirt controversial social issues through vaguely worded laws intended to leave the definition of their meaning to administrators and judges. In these instances, the primary effect of the legislation is not to solve a particular problem but to provide a structure within which agencies and ultimately the courts can fashion remedial approaches.

Entanglement in the thickets of social controversy has forced the courts to move beyond their power of judicial review, which enables them to declare legislative or executive acts unconstitutional and thus void. In extreme cases, judges have gone as far as to engage in quasi-administrative day-to-day monitoring of explosive and complex situations in order to ensure compliance with court orders. The ultimate sanction behind judicial orders has been the power of the courts to hold individuals and institutions in contempt. Generally, however, judges have tried to avoid such direct confrontations and have attempted to achieve community support through political negotiations and the use of analytical studies of problems. In this approach, activist judges have utilized the ideas of reformist thinkers who have stressed the value of judicial sensitivity to community interests and the findings of social analysis. Nevertheless, judicial activity has not provided policy analysts the degree of support that might be expected. Instead, the courts' use of policy analysis in their attempts to resolve social problems has often illustrated the uncertainties that can arise from the interplay of analysis and values even in a relatively rational and formal institutional context.

The adversary process has been both a boon and a danger to policy analysis. It has had the advantage of increasing the demand for analysts, as neither side in litigation wishes to be found to be using flawed analysis and at the same time each hopes to be able to point out problems in its opponent's position. As Serge Taylor has noted, the "residual uncertainty" as to what courts might do has increased the analyst's status and leverage within agencies.[1] Thus the technically oriented analyst who wishes to avoid the partisan aspects of policy formulation can still have considerable influence simply by insisting that certain issues have to be examined in order to protect the agency's position should it become involved in litigation. Similarly, an analyst's best strategy within an agency is to provide his or her superiors with thorough and complete analysis so that agency spokesmen do not find themselves caught unprepared by their adversaries.

On the other side of the coin, the adversary nature of the judicial process seems to encourage the role of analyst as advocate and in this respect to strain the integrity of policy analysis as a profession. The free-wheeling, emotional nature of many American trials poses one of the more obvious challenges to the policy analyst. For attorneys dedicated to winning for their clients, the rules of the game are extremely loose, and policy analysts can easily be drawn into this orientation. Taylor suggests that "the mere anticipation that the other side will act to maximize its chances of prevailing on the policy issue, rather than to ascertain the evidence, may maintain a vicious circle in which both sides play fast and loose with the evidence."[2] Even the most reputable analysts, or professionals, can be moved to make arguments and statements that, in the heat of the courtroom drama and the opportunities provided by the media, deviate from their carefully considered conclusions.

Approaches to Legal Reasoning

From the turn of the century until 1937, the nation's courts were dominated by a conception of legal reasoning based on formal, abstract constitutional doctrines that tended to favor the interests of corporate property over those of social reformers. Drawing heavily on John Dewey's pragmatic ideas, reformers argued that judges should move from reliance on abstract constitutional principles to concern for the concrete effects of their decisions in human lives. Probably chief among the academic critics was Roscoe Pound, dean of Harvard Law School from 1916 to 1936.

Pound adapted Dewey's philosophical ideas into what he termed "sociological jurisprudence" and urged judges to recognize that, instead of objectively "finding" the law, they were engaged in making it. Sociological jurisprudence was a movement "for the adjustment of principles and doctrines to the human conditions they are to govern rather than to assumed first principles; for putting the human factor into the central place and relegating logic to its true position as an instrument."[3] Rather than shield themselves behind legal abstractions, judges should consciously undertake an equitable balancing of the needs of social interests through "continually more efficacious social engineering."[4] In this effort, they would replace the artificial logic of the legal syllogism with the findings of social science analysis. Pound urged courts to establish laboratories and reference sources for social science research that could be used to provide judges with accurate data on the social contexts of their cases and the effects of their decisions.

Although Pound stressed the need for empirical data to inform judicial decisions and criticized abstract natural-law doctrines, he remained convinced of the importance of general social norms in judging. The Legal Realist school, however, discounted the importance of tradition and normative standards in deciding cases. As G. Edward White has asserted, "A case, for Realists, was an autonomous entity whose doctrinal significance might well be confined to its own factual context."[5] Legal Realists, such as Jerome Frank, rejected the influence of judicial precedent and guiding legal principles in court decisions, arguing instead that judges should act on a case-by-case basis that left each case governed by the facts and issues specific to it. Despite the fact that in the 1930s Pound separated himself from the Realists because they devalued precedent and the essential normative elements of the law, by 1940 Legal Realism was the dominant form of jurisprudence in American law schools.[6] This development coupled with the Supreme Court's 1937 retreat from constitutional formalism in the face of FDR's Court-packing threat marked a level of achievement for reformist legal thinkers that set the stage for greater judicial activism. Realism provided a conceptual basis for reformist courts to attack social evils, but its focus on particular facts and issues evaded larger questions not only about normative standards but also about the essential character of institutional processes.[7]

Sources of Judicial Activism

During the 1950s, the activist beliefs of reformist jurisprudence began to be implemented by America's courts under the guidance of a Supreme Court headed by Chief Justice Earl Warren. Social analysis became an important input into judicial decisions. Through the opinions of the Warren Court, the nation's courtrooms became refuges for a wide variety of interests that could not obtain satisfactory relief in the political arenas of the policy process.

Racial Desegregation
Among the grievances brought before the nation's courts, racial discrimination came to be seen as the most blatant constitutional failing of America's elected officials. The Warren Court's decisions in this area constructed constitutional bases for increased judicial activism and served as examples of the judicial application of sociological jurisprudence. In the famous *Brown* v. *Board of Education*[8] decision, Chief Justice Warren drew on both legal precedent and social science research to support his ruling that racial segregation in public education was unconstitutional. In particular, he argued that regardless of the tangible equality of the racially segregated schools, social analysis had established that racial segregation in and of itself had damaging effects on black children, and his famous footnote 11[9] invoked psychological and sociological studies for documentation. Whether the Court was persuaded by the social science data or inserted it merely for additional support, its appearance in the decision demonstrated the emergent influence of a jurisprudence and reformist philosophy first articulated in the early decades of the century. Moreover, concern for the social consequences of the decision at hand was to be characteristic of Warren Court opinions in the areas of religion, reapportionment, criminal rights, and poverty, as well as that of racial discrimination. The definition of problems in these areas and the articulation of the routes toward their amelioration were to fall heavily on the shoulders of students of social analysis.

The Supreme Court's decision in *Brown* v. *Board of Education* was a momentous event in American history and as such plainly radical rather than incremental in nature. Nevertheless, the impact of the constitutional doctrine propounded by the Warren Court was to be tempered markedly by its follow-up decision *Brown* v. *Board of Education II*,[10] where it in effect returned desegregation policy to the realm of incrementalism. In this decision, Chief Justice Warren emphasized the differences in local conditions and the proximity of the district courts to these conditions. Thus, the Court ordered the district courts that had originally heard the cases grouped under the *Brown* decision to monitor implementation of that decision. In this effort, Warren instructed the district courts to utilize their "equity" jurisdiction, an attribute of judicial power that allowed these courts broad flexibility in effectuating the High Court's ruling. Finally, Warren urged that enforced compliance with the *Brown* decision proceed "with all deliberate speed," a phrase interpreted by many as a signal that desegregation should move slowly.

There are at least three major ways in which the Supreme Court's early desegregation decisions facilitated and encouraged vastly increased judicial intervention in social issues. In a purely legal sense, they provided strong precedents from which federal courts could claim authority to invoke remedial powers where constitutional rights appeared to have been violated. Second, the decisions gave greater legitimacy to the analyses of social scientists. This development had less obvious but perhaps more far-reaching ramifications than the legal standards of the *Brown* decision, for it opened the possibility that the basis for legal standing to pursue social issues could be broadened considerably. Essentially, if social problems were to become a concern of the judicial system, then courts could be expected to be much more sensitive to the existence of these problems as defined by social scientists, who, on the whole, have not been hesitant in locating instances of social injustice. Finally, through the desegregation decisions the activities of the National Association for the Advancement of Colored People (NAACP) and a number of other groups confirmed the effectiveness of organization as a means of influencing favorably the judicial process and, ultimately, the supreme law of the land as enunciated by the nation's highest court.

Procedural Changes

In succeeding decades, these activist ramifications of the early desegregation decisions were reinforced by the Supreme Court's liberalization of the requirements of standing to sue, the basis on which a litigant may claim an injury that allows him or her to bring a case before a court.

The Court's receptivity to new kinds of cases has given it a much greater role in establishing rules and values for society. Interest groups have also gained in influence as the Court has shown a greater willingness to consider their analyses of social problems.

The growth of interventionist government, largely at the urging of one generation of social reformers, ironically created serious concern among a later generation of reformers. This later generation looked to an activist judiciary to correct injustices that they argued were created by the welfare state. These views were articulated forcefully in Charles A. Reich's 1964 *Yale Law Journal* article "The New Property." Reich contended that government largesse had created a new form of property that was almost wholly dependent on bureaucratic discretion. In their efforts to invoke governmental aid in the cause of social change, previous reformers had "summoned up a doctrine monstrous and oppressive"[11] that, in effect, made much of society dependent on administrative discretion for economic profit, or, more seriously, for bare subsistence. The administrative process was "characterized by uncertainty, delay, and inordinate expense; to operate within it requires considerable know-how."[12] Those with sufficient resources could eventually manipulate the system to their benefit; the individual indigent, dependent on welfare and other forms of assistance, remained at the mercy of the bureaucracy.

Reich argued that it was time that government assistance be treated as a form of property protected by adequate legal procedures: "There is no justification for the survival of arbitrary methods where valuable rights are at stake."[13] The inequities of the administrative process should be replaced with judicially enforced due process protections that ensure the application of fair procedures before governmental benefits are terminated. In essence, Reich was saying that the courts should allow standing to individuals and organizations to enable them to obtain protection from administrative bias and arbitrariness, and his article has been credited with influencing the Supreme Court's move in this direction. In particular, his views seem to have found support in *Goldberg* v. *Kelly* (1970),[14] where the Court explicitly rejected the privileges view of governmental aid in favor of one in which an indigent's welfare assistance was defined as a legal right that could not be terminated without that person being afforded proper due process protections.

Although the Court drew back from granting carte blanche procedural protections to those receiving governmental assistance, it continued to widen the basis for gaining access to the federal courts. By 1976, Karen Orren could announce the existence of a markedly more flexible standing test that appeared to stem from a "pronounced disenchantment" with administrative processes among Supreme Court justices.[15] Standing under the restrictive "aggrieved party" standard of the Administrative Procedure Act of 1946 had required a demonstration that a specific statutory or constitutional right had been infringed by governmental action. Thirty years later, this standard had been widened into a judicially protected "zone of interests" that allowed a range of organized interests, including environmentalists, consumer groups, and historical preservationists, to claim the infliction of noneconomic, intangible injuries from agency decisions as the basis for standing to sue.

Orren was especially concerned about the courts' willingness to accept broad definitions of what constituted legally redressable injury. Often these were formulated by organizations posing as representatives for whole segments of the population, such as consumers or nature lovers. The justices' generosity toward the pleas of organized interests raised the distinct possibility that the particularistic definitions of social problems formulated by these interests would lead to the legal imposition of their narrow normative standards on society at large.

Organized Interests
In the judicial arena, organized interests have not been able to establish the kind of direct access and pervasive influence found in other areas of the policy process, but they have become an essential ingredient in the formulation of policy by the courts. Simply in terms of the financial resources necessary to pursue a case, particularly where social issues are concerned, group organization is necessary. Groups have also developed strategies that help to ensure favorable court decisions. Chief among these is the use of test cases that are carefully selected because they present the facts and issues in a light favorable to the group's position. Often these cases are filed as class action suits, making them, in essence, suits on behalf of all individuals similarly affected by the governmental action or inaction at issue and positioning the interest-group litigant as spokesman for these people. Where a class action suit is allowed, the court's decision automatically applies to all persons disadvantaged by the governmental policy, not just to the particular litigants to the case. These strategies, in conjunction with the greater powers exercised by courts and their willingness to consider social science data, have provided organized interests with important power over society.[16]

With the careful use of policy analysis, interests can locate and define social problems of concern to them. They are then able to use organizational resources and legal skills to introduce these data into the courtroom in an effort to obtain a ruling defining and expanding their rights more effectively. An excellent example of this approach was provided by the Supreme Court's consideration of a challenge to capital punishment based primarily on statistical analyses of the racial application of the death sentence.[17] The plaintiff's contention was that because proportionately more blacks than whites received the death sentence, its use must be seen as racially motivated. The Court declined to base its consideration of the constitutionality of capital punishment on these statistical data or their general social extrapolation.

Examples of Judicial Activism: Social and Technological Change

Other examples of judicial activism can be drawn from the fields of public education and institutionalized care. In these areas, it became evident that group efforts to expand rights entailed a significant expansion of the power of the federal courts in society. As the courts exercised this power, they became embroiled in political battles with elected officials and state bureaucracies that quickly overshadowed the input of policy analysts.

After having used the judicial process successfully to obtain the *Brown* decision, civil rights groups maintained continued litigation pressure on local school boards to ensure movement toward integration. The resulting court decisions led to step-by-step increases in the power of lower federal courts. The key decision in this respect was *Green v. County School Board* (1968).[18] Declaring its impatience with the pace of school desegregation, the Supreme Court in *Green* specified that school boards had an affirmative duty to act to remedy conditions of segregation and that district court judges should be more aggressive in seeing that school boards acted constructively. In Bernard Schwartz's opinion:

> Under *Green,* the district courts were now expressly vested with the affirmative duty to supervise the operation of desegregation plans. The clear implication was that they should do whatever they deemed necessary to ensure that those plans proved effective in practice. Discharge of the judicial duty here might well involve the courts in the intimate details of school administration.[19]

The Court further decreed that lower-court judges had the authority to retain jurisdiction of a desegregation case until they were certain that segregation stemming from deliberate state policy had been eliminated.

Racial Integration

The *Green* decision precipitated a flurry of renewed activity by civil rights groups. In Charlotte, North Carolina, District Court Judge James B. McMillan received a petition asking that the local school board be ordered to undertake an effective effort to desegregate the Charlotte-Mecklenburg School District.[20] Although as a prominent member of the North Carolina bar McMillan had publicly stated his skepticism of forced integration, the plaintiffs' analyses and use of precedent convinced him of the illegality of the existing situation and of his responsibility to act. Despite repeated orders from Judge McMillan, however, the Charlotte-Mecklenburg School Board refused to come forward with a desegregation plan that met constitutional standards. Finally, Judge McMillan designated Dr. John A. Finger, Jr., an expert on school desegregation policy, to formulate an acceptable plan. In February 1970, Judge McMillan ordered the school board by the end of the school year to implement the Finger Plan, which provided for busing 10,000 students daily to achieve racially balanced schools. Although the public outcry against Judge McMillan's order was tremendous, the Supreme Court in *Swann* v. *Charlotte-Mecklenburg* (1971)[21] unanimously affirmed it, thereby imposing a judicial solution on a heated public policy debate being waged throughout the nation.

Despite the volatility of the busing issue, within a reasonably short time after the *Swann* decision, Judge McMillan obtained compliance from the school board. In this he was aided considerably by the good offices of the Citizens Advisory Group, which acted as liaison between the school board and the court and served to soften for the school board members the impact of judicial directives. In 1974, Judge McMillan approved a revised integration plan from the school board, and in 1975 he withdrew from supervision of the school board, ending seven years of litigation.

Meanwhile, in Boston, District Court Judge Wendell Arthur Garrity continued to have difficulty bringing the school board into constitutional compliance on the issue of racial balance in the schools.[22] In the spring of 1972, Judge Garrity had begun hearings in *Morgan* v. *Hennigan*,[23] a case with which he was to be closely involved for the next decade. During this period, continued opposition by the school board to judicially mandated integration led Judge Garrity to assume administrative control of the Boston schools, an action that involved him in the day-to-day management of the public schools to a degree unprecedented in the federal judiciary. As school superintendent, Judge Garrity set school hours and supervised the hiring and firing of personnel. At a more mundane level of detail, he found himself ordering twelve MacGregor basketballs and six Acme Tornado whistles for South Boston. Concerned also with students' creature comforts, Judge Garrity cautioned those converting elementary schools into middle-level schools to take care to see that the urinals were elevated.[24] But despite prodigious efforts and extraordinary attention to detail, Judge Garrity was never able to obtain the community support necessary to make racial balance a constructive educational experience in Boston.

Following testimony on the question of racial discrimination in the Boston schools, Judge Garrity in June 1974 issued a 152-page opinion finding that deliberate discrimination by the school board existed. Then, as an interim implementation measure, he adopted a state Department of Education plan that, like Judge McMillan's plan, had drawn on the input of policy specialist Dr. Finger. This plan mandated widespread busing, but most serious was its attempt to combine the students from the white working-class South Boston area with those from the black Roxbury area. The intense opposition in these areas to the integration plan led to rioting that forced Governor Francis Sargent in October to call out the National Guard to restore order.

During this time, Judge Garrity established a masters' committee to recommend to the court a long-term plan for integration of the schools. J. Anthony Lukas sees this group of six Bostonians as being guided primarily by Edward McCormick, a prominent Boston attorney and politician. After holding extensive public hearings, the masters' committee presented Judge Garrity with a plan that they believed was constitutionally adequate and had broad community acceptance. Judge Garrity, however, rejected important parts of the plan, increasing the number of children to be bused and retaining the combination of the Roxbury and South Boston areas. The result was continued community bitterness and opposition and white flight from the public schools, with the trend line pointing toward a public school system that would soon be predominantly black and poor in its student composition.[25]

Although the contexts and results differed markedly, the desegregation actions of Judges McMillan and Garrity contained parallels that spoke to the policy future of the federal courts. Both drew heavily on analyses of education specialists, both utilized interim groups of community leaders, and both, with varying degrees of success, sought community support. Most important, however, the racial desegregation decisions allowed these judges and others throughout the federal system to develop an arsenal of tools and techniques for enhancing their effectiveness as policy implementors. Essentially, federal judges were creating an image of judicial power that was to carry over into other areas of judicial concern. The opportunities for such intervention increased as courts responded sympathetically to analytical findings used to support legal efforts to expand the already broadened criteria for standing to sue.

Other Areas of Social Distress

The impetus that the racial desegregation cases provided for judicial intervention into other areas was illustrated exceptionally well by the record of

District Court Judge Frank Johnson of the Middle District of Alabama, whose career has been ably chronicled by Tinsley Yarbrough.[26]

In important ways, Judge Johnson's early initiatives in school desegregation were to foreshadow his attempts to reform the state's prisons and mental institutions. What is particularly fascinating about Judge Johnson's approach to social change is the fact that he was not eager to invoke the extensive powers of his position. He acted at an early date to remedy segregated schools in central Alabama, but he never advocated the idea of forced busing of students. And although he fought bitter battles with the authorities of Alabama, he remained throughout reluctant to use the court's contempt power to gain compliance. Judge Johnson was effective as a force for social change because he was intelligent, patient, politically astute, and sensitive to the positions of administrators and the community at large.

In March 1967, Judge Johnson authored the decree of a three-judge federal court requiring the end of segregated schools in Alabama. The objective was clear, but the means adopted by the judges were gradual. The judges met weekly with school district officials from around the state, monitoring their progress toward integration and moving them toward greater compliance. In the meantime, the judges were gradually tightening the standards to be met. In this manner, Judge Johnson and his brethren moved Alabama's schools toward integration with a minimum of violence. Equally important in light of his later actions, Judge Johnson's firmness and good judgment won him the respect of the federal appellate courts, and they were subsequently willing to grant him a great deal of flexibility in his approaches to other problems.

Judge Johnson's movement into Alabama's mental health institutions began in earnest in October 1970, with the case of *Wyatt* v. *Stickney*.[27] His exercise of judicial discretion during the litigation of this case was nothing short of sweeping. Although the case was originally filed on behalf of employees who were being cut from the payroll in mental institutions, Judge Johnson informed the attorneys at an early date that he was more interested in the rights of the patients. As a result, the attorneys quickly transformed the case into a class action suit on behalf of the patients in the state's three mental institutions. In March 1971, Judge Johnson issued a preliminary finding holding that the state's mental patients had a constitutional right to "adequate treatment," a position for which he had almost no supporting precedents.[28] Thus, Judge Johnson refocused the case away from the claims of the original plaintiffs and then almost by simple assertion created constitutional rights for the new plaintiffs. After a series of hearings featuring testimony by many experts in the field, the judge issued a comprehensive order with detailed standards to be met by the three mental institutions. To monitor implementation of his order, he established a human rights committee for each institution. The Fifth Circuit Court of Appeals upheld Judge Johnson's decision, and the Supreme Court denied review of the case, making *Wyatt* v. *Stickney* a major constitutional precedent for standards in mental institutions.

Judge Johnson's forays into the Alabama prison system had a firmer constitutional basis than his opinion for the state's mental patients, as there were numerous precedents where federal judges had intervened on behalf of state prisoners. After extensive hearings, conditions in the prisons were found to be so bad that the state conceded that they violated the constitutional prohibition against cruel and unusual punishment and agreed to work with the plaintiffs in formulating a plan that would pass constitutional muster. In January 1976, Judge Johnson issued a comprehensive order detailing the standards to be met in the Alabama prisons. Following his *Wyatt* approach, he established a human rights committee to monitor state compliance with his order. Governor George Wallace, apparently taken aback by the scope of Judge Johnson's ruling, denied that he had given the state's attorneys the authority to enter into a consent agreement. Although he apologized for his public statements that federal judges should be given barbed-wire enemas, the governor nonetheless proceeded to appeal Judge Johnson's order. Ultimately, the Circuit Court of Appeals upheld much of the judge's opinion. It did not, however, support his specification of space requirements for prisoners or his order that prisoners be provided with educational or vocational training opportunities. It also disagreed with his use of a human rights committee, arguing that a single master, who could monitor but not intervene in prison affairs, would be more appropriate.

Judge Johnson recognized early in his reform efforts the importance of maintaining continuing communication with the parties to a case and with the political system. He utilized extensively his ties with the "old boy network" in Alabama politics that went back to his law school days with Governor Wallace and other leading politicians. Nonetheless, he constantly encountered opposition from the state's bureaucracy, who were often backed by Governors George or Lurleen Wallace. His human rights committees met particular difficulties in attempting to work with the Alabama prison authorities, and at one point Judge Johnson had to threaten to reclassify each prisoner personally before cooperation was achieved. Only when George Wallace stepped down from office did Judge Johnson face a more amenable political climate. At that point, Wallace's successor, Governor Forest F. James, asked Judge Johnson to appoint him receiver for both the mental health system and the prison system, a request that the judge quickly granted. This development reflected Governor James's desire to remove the federal courts from a supervisory capacity. But, more significantly, it suggested that the state finally had a chief executive prepared to accept responsibility for providing adequate care for the less fortunate.[29]

The concerted opposition of Alabama officials to Judge Johnson's criticisms of their prisons and mental institutions reflected the fact that as judges have moved from dealing with clear constitutional wrongs involving race to social problems that are often vaguely defined and poorly understood, they have faced increasingly effective opposition from other policy bodies. These struggles have at times called into question the capabilities of the courts as policy makers. In essence, federal district courts have found it far more difficult to direct large state bureaucracies and state legislatures than to command the compliance of local school boards. Robert A. Burt has argued that "no matter what judges do, they have only limited capacity to command obedience from these mammoth bureaucratic enterprises charged with complex social welfare functions."[30] Not only are the state bureaucracies large and complex, but they are peopled by experts in their fields who have survived and prospered as much through their political skills as through their knowledge. Thus, at the state level, the courts have encountered political alliances and relationships similar to those that have grown so powerful at the national level. These coalitions proved particularly resistant to the efforts of federal judges in New York and Pennsylvania, who, when they moved into the mental health area, found the effective implementation of their decisions to be exceedingly elusive.

In New York, U.S. District Court Judge Orin Judd responded to petitions asking the courts to intervene to reform the horrible conditions in the Willowbrook State School with a preliminary injunction that attempted to provide an interim remedy until formal judicial proceedings had run their course.[31] After a lengthy trial and before Judge Judd could issue a final decision, Governor Hugh Carey and the State of New York entered into a consent decree, agreeing to meet court-imposed standards. Of these, the most substantive was that Willowbrook was to be reduced from over 5000 inmates to 250 within six years. To monitor the changes at Willowbrook and to make recommendations, Judge Judd appointed a review panel. Almost immediately, the review panel met opposition from the New York State

Department of Mental Hygiene. This conflict continued until April 1980, when the state legislature eliminated the funding for the review panel, and Governor Carey refused to act to provide other monies. For his inaction, Governor Carey was held in contempt by Judge John Bartels, who had assumed responsibility for the litigation on the death of the previous judge, Orin Judd, in 1976. The Second Circuit Court of Appeals overruled Judge Bartel's contempt citation, however, holding that a federal court could not force the governor to act contrary to state law. Subsequently, Judge Bartels appointed a Special Master to monitor the Willowbrook situation. The transition from Willowbrook to its professionally acceptable successor, the Staten Island Developmental Center, was finally completed in September 1987.

In Pennsylvania, District Court Judge Raymond Broderick was also facing sustained obstruction from state officials in his efforts to deal with the problems at Pennhurst State School and Hospital. Following a trial of thirty-two days in which he heard testimony from numerous witnesses, Judge Broderick, in December 1977, concluded that the only effective remedy for the conditions at Pennhurst was its closure.[32] He ordered the institution closed and its residents transferred, most to community residences. The state, however, maintained that he did not have the authority to order closure or to specify the criteria for Pennhurst's termination as a mental institution. The result was a series of challenges to Judge Broderick's orders, several of which reached the Supreme Court. Of particular note here is the fact that the High Court tended to support the state's position, but the Third Circuit Court of Appeals and Judge Broderick were able to interpret its decisions narrowly and thus maintain pressure on the state.

Following his original decision, Judge Broderick had appointed a Special Master to monitor the closing of Pennhurst. At one point, emboldened by New York State's action, the Pennsylvania legislature, with the public support of the head of the state welfare department, halted funding for the Special Master's office. This action brought a quick contempt citation from Judge Broderick against the state department head. The citation was affirmed by the court of appeals, and the state legislature renewed funding for the Special Master's office. Apparently the legislature empathized with Georgia Governor Marvin Griffin, who, when asked how he felt about contempt citations, is reputed to have responded, "Being in jail sorta crimps a governor's style."[33] Although no one went to jail in Pennsylvania, the state, for a variety of actions and inactions, eventually was assessed over $1 million in fines for contempt of court.

Finally, in August 1982, Judge Broderick ended the office of Special Master and assumed direct control of the case himself. Numerous hearings and orders followed with the judge continually pointing to the state's recalcitrance. In July 1983, the state and the private plaintiffs to the case reached an agreement to close Pennhurst by July 1986; although this deadline was not met, by the fall of 1986, Pennhurst was close to being emptied of inmates.

Judicial Social Activism in Perspective
As the courts have moved from the protection of racial rights into other categories of social policy, questions have arisen as to the institutional capability of the judiciary to deal effectively with controversial policy questions.[34] Some of the difficulties that the courts have faced have stemmed from the essentially political nature of the problems with which they have found themselves dealing, as with Judge Johnson in Alabama. In contrast to the frequent inaction or ambiguous decisions of the electorally responsible parts of the policy process, courts can issue concrete decisions. But they then encounter the problems of institutional and procedural fragmentation in the *implementation* of their decisions. Furthermore, as administrative and legislative policy makers become more adept at dragging their collective feet in response to judicial edicts, it will become even more difficult for the courts to achieve constructive compliance. In this kind of context, judges themselves are almost forced to move from behind the bench into the policy melee to monitor the implementation of their decisions.

In addition to political obstacles to judicial policy making, the forms and procedures of the judicial process itself limit the effectiveness of the courts. A lawsuit is a formal, often excruciatingly detailed process that limits a court to the initiative of the parties and to the facts and arguments presented by them. A court may, of course, allow other interested parties to participate in argument as *amicus curiae* (friend of the court) and may request additional information, but a judge's sources of usable information remain severely limited in comparison to those available to other policy-making bodies. As a consequence, in most cases, the vision of the court is bounded by the parameters of an issue as presented by the adversary parties, and the broader social and political aspects of a question receive little or no formal consideration. Phillip J. Cooper has noted a tendency for defendants in cases calling for remedial decrees to narrow a judge's perspective by stipulating to the facts or refusing to present a defense. Not only do these tactics deny the judge the "validity check of a balanced adversary process" but they also weaken or dilute the record on which the judge's decision will be based.[35] This narrow focus is reinforced by the natural tendency of judges, as the products of a particular kind of educational and socialization process, to think of issues in terms of rights rather than in terms of alternative ways of resolving complex problems and reconciling conflicting interests. The backgrounds of judges and the institutionalized focus of the judicial process encourage courts to think in terms of the apportionment of blame and the application of proper constitutional remedies at a time when they are being drawn into policy issues more appropriately dealt with in a broader, more flexible fashion.[36]

Efforts by Judge Johnson and the courts in New York and Pennsylvania to reform state institutions were, like the attacks on racial segregation, guided initially by moral outrage. In these cases, the conditions challenged were so bad that the parties to the litigation agreed to their lack of constitutional validity. Consequently, the findings and suggestions of policy analysts that became part of the judicial record did not receive the scrutiny that they might otherwise have. Opposition by state bureaucracies to judicial remedies grew only when the extent and costs of these remedies, based heavily on the recommendations of specialists in the areas, emerged.

In these cases, the problematic role of the analyst in the judicial process became apparent. Judge Johnson relied extensively on expert opinions in his detailed implementation orders and in fact attempted to have academic specialists participate in the actual reform of the Alabama prison system.[37] These opinions and efforts were not well received by those shouldering the tasks of day-to-day administration. The confrontation was not simply one of uncaring vested interests versus humane reformers. Judge Johnson's original order detailing cell size, for example, specified a standard nowhere met in the Alabama prison system. Judge Broderick's order closing Pennhurst was based on testimony by those favoring community placement, a position soon challenged by other specialists in the field. These professionals argued persuasively that for some mentally disabled, institutionalization was more effective and humane.[38]

Although the orders rendered by the judges in these cases had legitimate roots in the professional literature, the original court cases themselves and the ensuing hearings encouraged the full play of the analyst as advocate. A variety of professional associations and reform-oriented advocacy groups quickly entered the various legal efforts. Believing that they were engaged in an adversary process, these groups naturally presented their arguments and data in as strong a fashion as possible. When the defendants agreed to many of their challenges, the plaintiffs' views survived in the judicial forum without the tempering, or moderating, effects that active opposition might have had. The courts in turn were denied the wider consideration of approaches that more confrontational interaction might have provided.

The restricted focus of the judiciary makes it vulnerable to exploitation by organized interests. To enhance their chances for judicial success, organizations can employ the services of policy analysts to locate and define judicially cognizable problems that will widen the range of issues on which they can litigate. Thus, in the 1970s, the Sierra Club undertook to challenge every Forest Service Unit Plan environmental impact statement in that agency's California region.[39] Because of their ability to initiate and monitor cases throughout the country, interests are able to select for sustained litigation those that appear to present the most blatant violations of constitutional rights. The combination of greater use of policy analysis, increased organizational activity, and wider reliance on the test-case strategy has often left the courts responding to "worst possible case" types of behavior. Constitutional remedies fashioned to deal with these situations are then imposed by the courts on everyone living or working in similar conditions. As Taylor has noted, the effects can be unsettling to agencies.

> A court aroused by a particularly egregious case which it regards as "typical," or at least as unacceptably frequent, may therefore operate with an incorrect theory of what caused the problem, and in all likelihood also with an incorrect theory of how to remedy it. In its zeal to fashion a remedy, a court may disrupt agency policy and procedures in ways that the agency regards as much worse than reversing a particular decision, or sometimes even the general policy at issue.[40]

Effective implementation of judicial policy has also become a more serious problem as the courts have intervened in a greater range of social issues. Part of the difficulty appears to be conceptual, and part is clearly institutional. On the former point, Bruce Ackerman argues that within the context of a welfare, interventionist state, activist lawyers operating from a Realist conceptual framework are engaged in an unending quest for reform. In his view, "the activist lawsuit is but a chapter in a never-ending story of the polity's struggle with an ongoing problem.... A final judgment no longer suggests that everything worth saying has been said, only that it is best, all things considered, to say no more for a time."[41] In institutional terms, judges are limited in their ability to ensure effective implementation of their decisions because in most instances they must proceed on a case-by-case approach that depends on litigation being brought by those adversely affected. Conceptually and institutionally, courts are oriented toward piecemeal adjudication of issues that may never reach areas of policy difficulty where interest or resources for litigation are lacking.

The conclusions suggested here are not altered by the fact that some judges have undertaken day-to-day comprehensive monitoring of the implementation of their decisions. Any extensive imitation of these efforts would put an unbearable strain on the resources of the nation's courts, which are already backlogged in many areas. Even in instances where comprehensive orders have been issued, the presiding judges have often found themselves continuously modifying them in response to petitions brought by the litigants.

Judicial Response to Technological Change

When the courts have moved into policy areas involving the problems caused by technological change, they have faced difficulties as serious as those encountered in their efforts to effect social change. Where science and technology are concerned, judges carry the additional burden of lacking expertise in these areas. Somewhat surprisingly, the courts' attempts to resolve problems wrought by science and technology have made the need for values in rendering final decisions most obvious. In these contests, both sides have drawn heavily on analytical claims, and it has rapidly become apparent that policy analysis does not play ideological favorites. After examining the extensive use of cost-benefit analysis by the Corps of Engineers and the environmentalist groups in their court battles, Taylor concludes that everyone "now realizes that the issue is a value choice."[42] Faced with a lack of fundamental normative consensus and the rapid pace of scientific change, judges have been sorely pressed in their efforts to draw on their generalist backgrounds and a legal tradition based on gradual movement toward legal change to fashion workable accommodations to the demands of social interests. Their approaches to environmental issues provide examples of some of the problems raised by scientific and technological change.

In February 1972, the U.S. Environmental Protection Agency filed suit in the District Court of Minnesota against the Reserve Mining Company in Silver Bay, Minnesota.[43] Reserve Mining extracted iron ore north of Silver Bay, and at its Silver Bay plant on the shore of Lake Superior processed the ore into small pellets for shipment to Ohio steel plants. In this process, the taconite waste from which the iron ore was separated was dumped into

Lake Superior at the rate of 67,000 tons per day, creating a turbid layer estimated to be 37 miles wide, 3 miles long, and 100 to 300 feet deep. Before the trial began, the case received impetus from the discovery that the asbestos-like fibers from the taconite waste were in the drinking water of communities along Lake Superior, including that of Duluth, approximately 50 miles to the south. These fibers also were present in the air around Silver Bay. After a trial lasting 134 days over a nine-month period in which testimony was given by experts from both sides and from those appointed by the court, Judge Miles W. Lord found that Reserve Mining was creating a serious health hazard and issued an injunction ordering the plant to stop dumping waste into Lake Superior. This injunction was almost immediately stayed by the Eighth Circuit Court of Appeals.

Following lengthy negotiations at the appellate and district court levels, appeals to the court of appeals, and remands by that court back to Judge Lord for resolution of unresolved issues, Judge Lord in November 1975, without giving Reserve Mining opportunity to be heard, ordered the company to pay the City of Duluth $100,000 in damages. In his order, Judge Lord noted that "I have dispensed with the usual adversary proceedings here, because I simply do not have time to spend, as I did, nine months in hearing, six months of which was wasted by what I find now, and did find in my opinions, to be misrepresentations by Reserve Mining Company." [44] In January 1976, the Eighth Circuit Court of Appeals dissolved Judge Lord's order, returned the funds to the company, and took the unusual step of ordering Judge Lord removed from the case entirely. Finally, in May 1976, after over seven years of litigation and negotiations, Judge Lord's successor, Judge Edward J. Devitt, in a decision later affirmed at the appellate level, ordered Reserve Mining to pay over $1 million in fines and costs and to halt dumping in Lake Superior by 7 July 1977. [45]

The Reserve Mining case in many ways is a classic example of a clash of values, technology, and judicial procedure. Judge Lord, convinced of the danger of taconite dumping to human health, found himself frustrated by the tactics of the company and the lack of support from his court of appeals. At the same time, the evidence as to the imminent danger posed to communities by the fibers in their water was not strong. Although no one disputed the need for action, the real issue for the company was how soon it had to act to find an alternative means of disposing of its waste products. In this respect, Judge Lord, a man of strong convictions, appears to have been frustrated as much by the requirements of the legal process as by the tactics of the Reserve Mining Company.

Congress has also been slow to recognize the difficulties that scientific and technological change pose for judicial policy making. In the National Environmental Policy Act (NEPA) of 1969 Congress attempted to enlist policy analysts to inform and legitimize governmental decisions by requiring that government projects must be preceded by an acceptable environmental impact statement. The act is one instance of many where Congress fairly directly deferred the details of policy questions to the courts and administrators. In his examination of how the NEPA was implemented on the west coast, Taylor has shown the limitations of the adversary use of policy analysis in a judicial process lacking fundamental value consensus.

Congress's imposition of the environmental impact requirement reflected that body's belief that proper analysis of a project's effects would contribute to protection of the environment and to agreement as to an action's merit. In practice, however, its most important immediate consequence was that it was perceived by organizations intent on preventing environmental damage as another basis for litigation against governmental agencies such as the Forest Service and the Corps of Engineers. The ensuing lawsuits increased the demand for policy analysts both within and outside government. As the opposing interests clashed in the judicial arena, it soon became apparent that the courts were ill prepared and reluctant to engage in difficult scientific questions. The adversary employment of analytical findings did not necessarily contribute to greater clarification of issues or certainty as to the appropriate approaches toward their resolution.

The agencies often lost the early challenges to their environmental impact statements because the issues raised were largely procedural. As agencies became more careful about following the proper steps in preparing impact statements, environmentalists turned to questioning the accuracy of the statements. The agencies responded to this tack by preparing detailed analyses and extensive justifications for their proposals. During this phase of the struggle, the agencies were usually successful in court, primarily for two reasons. First, they were able to use their superior resources to "outmuscle" the private interest groups by providing elaborately documented and detailed analyses and by continuing cases through the various levels of judicial appeal. Second, the courts' unwillingness to delve into complex scientific areas prompted them to give credence to agency positions once they were satisfied that the appropriate procedural standards had been met.[46]

In their attempts to supervise adherence to the requirements of the NEPA, the courts found themselves in a highly technical area without a tradition of judicial precedents for guidance and acting under the authority of legislation lacking in precision. As laypersons in the scientific field, judges may have justifiably felt themselves on tenuous grounds deciding substantive environmental questions. But as students of the law, they were specialists in the demands of proper procedure. Thus, in aggressively holding agencies accountable to their own regulations and the requirements of the NEPA, the courts were drawing on their particular form of expertise to enhance the legitimacy of their decisions. Although the agencies have been largely successful on substantive issues, the willingness of the courts to act against them in the procedural area created considerable uncertainty as to how comprehensive their impact statements had to be. This, in turn, gave increased influence to the agencies' policy analysts, who were looked to not only for their methodological skills but also for their sense of what facets of an issue might have to be defended in court.

Fundamentally, the experiences of Judge Lord and those judges dealing with implementation of the NEPA point up once again the importance of normative consensus to effective policy. Scientific analysis, whether of the physical or social variety, cannot substitute for basic social agreement on a question nor can it by itself induce such agreement. The effectiveness of the courts in the area of racial discrimination rested not on the findings cited by Chief Justice Warren in footnote 11 but on the widespread belief in American society that it is wrong to treat people differently because of skin color. Despite historical and regional aberrations, the idea of equality of opportunity has constituted a basic normative position for Americans. But in the environmental field, and in other areas featuring rapid technological advances, such generally held norms do not yet exist, and, as William Lowrance has suggested, "Special contention arises where somewhat uncertain science intersects with somewhat uncertain values."[47] When the postulates of science have found agreement over time, there is little room for controversy, although changes will eventually occur even in these firmly held opinions. Alternatively, even without scientific certainty in an area, if a society has an accepted normative interpretation of the world that encompasses that area, there exists a basis for reaching acceptable solutions to problems. Unfortunately, the thrust in today's political culture has been toward greater normative divisiveness and the politicization of scientific findings.

With regard to the latter point, Hugh Heclo has argued that the attempt to paper over ideological divisions by relying more heavily on what appears to be administrative expertise can have serious consequences for public policy and policy analysis.[48] In the current policy context, analysis can quickly become another weapon in the political arsenals of competing camps, resulting in a cacophony of analytical findings and perspectives that deepens cynicism and apathy among the citizenry. Overanalysis of issues, then, may serve primarily to avoid basic normative divisions that are the real sources of difficulty in achieving workable policy. Lowrance has noted that it is much easier to use analytic techniques to identify problems and to demarcate inequities than it is to fashion fair solutions.[49] A culture fragmented by deep value differences renders the question of fairness even more difficult to resolve.

The Limits of Judicial Power

Although the Realist movement in American jurisprudence provided an important service by moving the judiciary toward an accommodation with the activist state, it failed to recognize the importance of the broader cultural and political contexts of judicial opinions. The procedures of the legal process and the reasoning of judges, in and of themselves, have not carried sufficient rational force to inculcate widespread obedience to judicial decrees when the courts have moved into judicially uncharted areas. Judge Johnson experienced the painful consequences of limited judicial power in such circumstances when mental institutions in Alabama met his client ceilings simply by releasing inmates. Subsequently, some were injured and others were left wandering around the community. On the intake side of the issue, the judge's client ceilings meant that those who could not get into state institutions were sent to community residences, where conditions were often much worse than those in the state institutions. While not facing state bureaucracies, Judge Lord found the corporate power of the Reserve Mining Company beyond his judicial means of control. Whether rightly or wrongly, the judicial contests between environmental groups and federal agencies in Taylor's study appear to have been decided ultimately in favor of those who could muster superior resources. Ackerman argues that judges trained in the Realist perspective have been oriented toward "thinking small, instead of placing their particular conflict within a larger framework of structural description."[50] Some of the judges examined here have moved beyond the facts of a specific case, but in doing so, they have had to engage in long, arduous struggles with more powerful political forces without clear conceptual guidance. Others have avoided the larger context of a case by retreating into procedural issues.

No matter what the theoretical justification used to support judicial

power in an activist state, courts are likely to continue to find their intervention into recently identified social problems to be hazardous to their status
in society. Taylor's view is that courts inevitably possess serious limitations
as policy makers in American politics: "Though courts certainly do make
policy, they do so without the kind of legitimacy that clothes the policy
choices of a legislature or elected executive. Nor, in confronting the agencies, do the courts possess a substitute legitimacy in the form of technical
expertise."[51] Not surprisingly, courts have been uniformly reluctant to invoke the draconian power of contempt against recalcitrant public officials
who have questioned their ventures into new areas of social policy.

The most successful policy-innovating judges have been those who have
displayed shrewdness in balancing their powers against powerful political
forces. Cooper argues that, for judges, "the truly hard choices come from
the effort to meet the elements of remedial adequacy while balancing those
demands against the need for limits to discretion, both the more formal
doctrinal constraints and the less formal judgmental factors associated with
a prudent sense of the court's relationship to the community and its administrative and elected officials."[52] This approach meshes closely with the in-
direction, or subterfuge, that Guido Calabresi has identified as a common
judicial maneuver in volatile cases where candor and directness would be
too socially divisive to allow for effective public policy.[53] If violations of
judicially defined rights were to be met on every front with swift and direct
judicial action, political and social repercussions would take an even greater
toll on judicial authority and status.

In terms of both definition and clarification, policy analysts have contributed greatly to an understanding of social problems. Their suggestions,
however, are no more final in the judicial process than in other arenas of decision making, and it would be unwise for judges to treat them as definitive.
Not only do the conclusions of scholars change, but the capability for dealing with problems changes. In this respect, courts often have a difficult time
adjusting to rapidly changing technology. Bartlett, for example, notes that
the methods for counting mineral fibers in drinking water at the outset of
the Reserve Mining controversy were crude and not very accurate. The
courts accepted this fact, and even though the ability to find such fibers
improved dramatically within a few years, their earlier judicial determination continued to carry weight.[54]

A more controversial example of the linkage of judicial policy to technology occurred in the *Roe* v. *Wade*[55] abortion decision, where Justice
Harry Blackmun based the right of a state to prohibit abortion on the point

in pregnancy at which medical science could keep a fetus alive. Since that decision has become the law of the land, it has become the focus of vehement ideological controversy. At the same time, medical technology has moved back the point of fetus viability outside the womb. This has left the Court with the difficult choice of remaining with the rule as originally formulated, even though improvements in science have undermined an important part of its basis, or of revising the law to conform with changing technology. In her dissent in *Akron* v. *Akron Center for Reproductive Health*, Justice Sandra Day O'Connor explained the problems with basing judicial rules concerning abortion on rapidly changing medical technology.

> [N]either sound constitutional theory nor our need to decide cases based on the application of neutral principles can accommodate an analytical framework that varies according to the "stages" of pregnancy, where those stages, and their concomitant standards of review, differ according to the level of medical technology available....
>
> The *Roe* framework, then, is clearly on a collision course with itself. As the medical risks of various abortion procedures decrease, the point at which the State may regulate for reasons of maternal health is moved further forward to actual childbirth. As medical science becomes better able to provide for the separate existence of the fetus, the point of viability is moved further back toward conception.[56]

Justice O'Connor's opinion has been widely cited by those opposing legalized abortions, but it serves also as a perceptive statement of the difficulties that policy analysis generally can pose for judicial rule making.

The inadequacies of the Realist position, the increased activism of judges, and the heightened debate among students of the courts as to the proper role of judicial power indicate that the time is ripe for the emergence of a more sophisticated notion of the political and normative facets of judging. Policy analysis will remain an important input into judicial policy, but it alone cannot and has not provided a firm foundation for judicial decisions. Analytical studies are subject to various interpretations and neverending methodological critiques. Moreover, even when a considerable degree of expert agreement has been achieved on a social issue, it rarely has any staying power. Thus, busing as a means to achieve integrated schools has come under severe criticism; community residences for the mentally disabled may have serious drawbacks and spillover effects; definitions of normality among psychologists and sociologists are in constant flux. Again, in the environmental area, the ramifications of governmental actions can be extended throughout the ecological chain and, perhaps, throughout the universe if one wishes to assume an expansive perspective. The question here is when to stop. What are the cost and other limits acceptable to society? Those attempting to integrate social and scientific analysis into judicial decisions must obtain a clearer conception of what these limits are. At this point, policy analysts have proven to be much better at diagnosing social problems than at outlining the consequences of remedies. This, of course, may always be the case, but a better understanding of their judicial role should contribute toward narrowing the gap between the two levels of analysis.

The really useful contribution of policy analysis occurs when some degree of normative agreement has first been reached. Robert A. Burt has in fact argued that the normative role of judging should be recognized as paramount in importance. In his view, judges should be seen as something like the high priests of the national conscience whose function is to force the holders of power to assume moral accountability for their actions. Judicial effectiveness from this perspective would be evaluated on the basis of a judge's "capacity to raise issues into high public visibility and force many different people ... to admit that they are morally responsible for an existing state of affairs...."[57] This moral catalyst view of judging has the merit of relieving judges of the heavier responsibilities of policy making and of drawing attention to fundamental issues, but it seems to run counter to the current trend of expecting courts to make definitive policy in a wide variety of areas.

In many respects, courts are now seen as essential components of the policy process. Interest groups regularly regard them as the next arena for contesting policies after the legislative and administrative processes have been exhausted. By loosening standing requirements and giving greater credence to the legal claims of groups, the Supreme Court has encouraged increased use of the courts for policy purposes. In too many instances, this stance has been reinforced by the irresponsibility of elected officials. The willingness of elected officials to allow Judge Johnson to deal with serious abuses of individual rights came to be known as the Alabama "punt syndrome." Similarly, in New York and Pennsylvania, public officials backed away from commitments or dragged their feet in making them when faced with tradeoffs between the demands of voting constituents and the needs of those too disabled to care for themselves. Again, school boards throughout the nation found it preferable to be prodded by court action rather than to take responsible, and probably electorally devastating, action on their own to implement constitutional requirements. The judges who have been most successful in implementing their decisions have been those who have candidly recognized the political nature of their position. Perhaps the most serious drawback to establishing the courts as merely an extension of the policy process is that this view opens the judiciary to the forces of relativism and fragmentation that have hampered the other branches of government.

Notes

1. Serge Taylor, *Making Bureaucracies Think* (Stanford: Stanford University Press, 1984), 239.

2. Ibid., 317.

3. Quoted in Edward McNall Burns, *Ideas in Conflict* (New York: Norton, 1960), 129.

4. Roscoe Pound, *An Introduction to the Philosophy of Law* (New Haven: Yale University Press, 1922), 99; see also Roscoe Pound, *Interpretations of Legal History* (New York: Macmillan, 1923), 152–59.

5. G. Edward White, *Tort Law in America* (New York: Oxford University Press, 1980), 73.

6. Ibid., 63.

7. Bruce A. Ackerman, *Reconstructing American Law* (Cambridge, Mass.: Harvard University Press, 1984), 5, 39–41.

8. 347 U.S. 483 (1954).

9. Ibid., at 49.

10. 349 U.S. 294 (1955).

11. Charles A. Reich, "The New Property," *Yale Law Journal* 73 (April 1964): 771.

12. Ibid., 765.

13. Ibid., 784.

14. 397 U.S. 254.

15. Karen Orren, "Standing to Sue: Interest Group Conflict in the Federal Courts," *American Political Science Review* 70 (September 1976): 723–41.

16. Based on his study of judicial intervention into social problems, Phillip Cooper argues that groups often become involved in judicial suits as the result of specific conditions that "trigger" a reaction rather than as the result of strategic planning. Phillip J. Cooper, *Hard Judicial Choices* (New York: Oxford University Press, 1988), 330–31.

17. *McCleskey* v. *Kemp*, 95 L. Ed. 2d 262 (1987).

18. 391 U.S. 430.

19. Bernard Schwartz, *Swann's Way* (New York: Oxford University Press, 1986), 61.

20. This discussion draws heavily on ibid.

21. 402 U.S. 1.

22. J. Anthony Lukas, *Common Ground* (New York: Knopf, 1985), 231–51; see also George R. Metcalf, *From Little Rock to Boston* (Westport, Conn.: Greenwood Press, 1983), 197–220.

23. 379 F. Supp. 410 (1974).

24. Lukas, *Common Ground*, 250.

25. Dye notes that of the 57,000 students remaining in Boston's public schools when Judge Garrity removed himself from the case in 1985, 27 percent were white. Thomas A. Dye, *Understanding Public Policy*, 6th ed. (Englewood Cliffs, N.J.: Prentice-Hall, 1987), 14.

26. Tinsley E. Yarbrough, *Judge Frank Johnson and Human Rights in Alabama* (University, Ala.: University of Alabama Press, 1981).

27. 325 F. Supp. 781 (1971).

28. Cooper discusses the legal and scholarly sources that provided support for Judge Johnson's opinion. Cooper, *Hard Judicial Choices*, 140–43, 174–75, 329.

29. The efforts of James, however, fell short and in 1983 Wallace again became governor, leading to another round of negotiations. See ibid., 198–200.

30. Robert A. Burt, "*Pennhurst*: A Parable," in *In the Interest of Children*, ed. Robert H. Mnookin (New York: Freeman, 1985), 350.

31. Material on Willowbrook is based on Mary Sue Rose, "Implementation of the Pennhurst Decision" (1984) and Maureen A. Lindberg, "The Willowbrook Consent Decree" (1984), Alfred University Graduate School, Alfred, N.Y.

32. Burt, "*Pennhurst*," 272.

33. Yarbrough, *Judge Frank Johnson*, 72.

34. Donald L. Horowitz, *The Courts and Social Policy* (Washington, D.C.: Brookings Institution, 1977).

35. Cooper, *Hard Judicial Choices*, 334.

36. Horowitz, *Courts and Social Policy*, 33–56, 264, 273.

37. Yarbrough, *Judge Frank Johnson*, 208.

38. Burt, "*Pennhurst*," 273.

39. Taylor, *Making Bureaucracies*, 203.

40. Ibid., 241.

41. Ackerman, *Reconstructing*, 35.

42. Taylor, *Making Bureaucracies*, 193.

43. Important sources for this case study are Robert V. Bartlett, *The Reserve Mining Controversy* (Bloomington: Indiana University Press, 1980); and Frank D. Schaumburg, *Judgment Reserved* (Reston, Va.: Reston Publishing, 1976). Bartlett notes that Schaumburg's book was supported by a public relations firm representing Reserve Mining. Bartlett, *Reserve Mining*, 225–26.

44. Quoted in Schaumburg, *Judgment*, 241–42.

45. *New York Times*, 5 May 1977, 35; 29 October 1977, 16.

46. Taylor, *Making Bureaucracies*, 187, 193, 232, 236. Focus on proper procedure was to characterize the Burger Court's treatment of agencies generally. See Alan B. Morrison, "Close Reins on the Bureaucracy: Overseeing the Administrative Agencies" in *The Burger Years*, ed. Herman Schwartz (New York: Penguin, 1988), 198–99.

47. William W. Lowrance, *Modern Science and Human Values* (New York: Oxford University Press, 1985), 137.

48. Hugh Heclo, "Issue Networks and the Executive Establishment," in *The New American Political System*, ed. Anthony King (Washington, D.C.: American Enterprise Institute, 1978), 118–21, 124.

49. Lowrance, *Modern Science*, 120.

50. Ackerman, *Reconstructing*, 74.

51. Taylor, *Making Bureaucracies*, 235.

52. Cooper, *Hard Judicial Choices*, 350.

53. Guido Calabresi, *A Common Law for the Age of Statutes* (Cambridge, Mass.: Harvard University Press, 1982), 172–73.

54. Bartlett, *Reserve Mining*, 212.

55. 410 U.S. 113 (1973).

56. 462 U.S. 416 (1983), at 452, 458.

57. Burt, "*Pennhurst*," 350.

Conclusion

The foregoing chapters indicate that policy analysis cannot be either optimally performed or optimally utilized in the highly decentralized and fragmented American polity of today. Institutional reform in the political system could enhance considerably the effectiveness of policy analysis. In this regard, a relatively small number of political scientists, elected officials, and journalists have called for fundamental reforms that aim at coordinating the American governmental system. Most of these ideas are inspired by institutions and procedures found in parliamentary democracies. Parliamentary systems typically give more emphasis to the coordination of governmental powers than does the American system. In addition to the need for basic institutional changes, we have also suggested the importance of a broad perspective on the part of policy analysts themselves. Better anticipation on their part of the effects of the policy process on analysis together with a greater awareness of the cultural values at stake are changes that can be made independently of the more cumbersome process of structural reform.

Structural Reform

Even though parliamentary-type reforms have little political support in America at present, a consideration of them is useful because most Americans are only dimly aware that there are other ways to organize free, democratic societies. Parliamentary proposals give a contrasting picture of how a more coordinated system might operate. We make no attempt here to present an encompassing review of such proposals; instead, we focus on two proposals that affect the election process, which lies at the heart of a working democracy.

170

Congressional Nomination of Presidential Candidates
Robert DiClerico and Eric Uslaner have proposed that the parties in Congress nominate presidential candidates.[1] In other words, the Democrats in the House and Senate would hold joint meetings and nominate their candidate for President. The Republicans would do the same. Such candidates, if elected, would begin office with a sizable base in Congress. The congressmen of the President's party, having nominated him, would have a larger personal stake in his success. To increase his chances of success, they would gravitate toward a nominee who not only appealed to the general public but who also had the skills to work with Congress.

For all these reasons, it can be argued that congressional nomination of presidential candidates would contribute to better coordination between the President and the two houses of Congress. Nevertheless, the idea goes against the grain of American political practice and preference. As noted earlier, American voters show high support for their individual congressmen, but low approval for Congress as a collective body. The latter suggests that they would be ill disposed to grant parties in Congress the collective responsibility of nominating presidential candidates.

Additionally, in most areas of politics and government, American voters have preferred greater direct access (which requires greater fragmentation) to better coordination of political institutions. The present, extremely fragmented nominations system consisting of numerous party primaries and party caucuses affords much greater public access to the presidential nomination process than would nominations confined to Congress.

Electing the President and Congress: The Team-Ticket Proposal
Separate elections of House members, Senate members, and the President lie at the heart of fragmentation among major power centers of the national government. The team-ticket proposal would knit these separate elections together in two distinct steps, which would probably require separate constitutional amendments.

The first step would be the simultaneous election of House members, Senate members, and the President every four years.[2] To achieve this, the two-year terms of House members would have to be lengthened and the six-year terms of Senate members shortened. Also "off year" Senate and House elections, which occur midway between presidential elections, would be eliminated.

Although simultaneous elections are time coordinated, they are still separate elections. Voters could still "split their ticket." For example, they could vote simultaneously for the Republican presidential candidate and the Democratic candidates for House and Senate. The second step of the team-ticket proposal would prevent this. Voters would be required to vote for a four-candidate party team consisting of the Republican candidates for President, vice-president, House, and Senate, or a team slate of the four Democratic candidates. Voters could not split their tickets.[3]

Perhaps the best place to begin coordinating a fragmented national government is in the minds of the voters. The team-ticket proposal would oblige voters first to think about, and then to choose, their national government as a coordinated unit. Team-ticket election would virtually end the typical phenomenon of the 1970s and 1980s: Presidents of one party facing Congresses in which one or both houses are dominated by the other party.

The team-ticket proposals, however, would reduce popular access to congressmen, and for that reason would have little appeal for voters. "Off year" congressional elections, for example, give voters an opportunity to focus more attention on how responsive their representative has been to state and local interests. Short, two-year terms for the House of Representatives serve much the same purpose.

Voters cherish their right to "split their tickets" in presidential election years for similar reasons. They may strongly prefer the presidential candidate of one party as a national leader, but they also want to be able to vote for the House or Senate candidate of the other party if he or she has been particularly good for the state or the district. The public expectation continues to be that the President will lead the nation, congressmen will represent their state and local districts, and coordination across the branches of the national government will somehow take care of itself.

These expectations have not been unrealistic from a historical perspective. Throughout most of American history, political fragmentation has existed side by side with economic growth and prosperity. Americans can hardly be reproached for perceiving a positive correlation between the two. Yet the fiscal crisis and other crises emerging may force on the American people a more critical understanding of the impact of an extremely fragmented political system on the making of public policy, both domestic and foreign. Most important, the merit of reform proposals focusing on the electoral process, in contrast to those attempting to straitjacket Congress, is that they move toward fundamental change in political relationships and attitudes.

Anticipating the Policy Process

Without major structural reforms, the policy process will continue to pose important challenges to the policy analyst. Many of these challenges can, however, be anticipated and strategies developed to lessen their impact. The primary prerequisite for the policy analyst is to have an understanding of the complexity of the policy process and an appreciation for the different perspectives and concerns that may be triggered by the recommendations under discussion.

One approach to decision making that has particular merit from the vantage point of the analyst is the PRINCE analysis developed by Michael K. O'Leary and William D. Coplin.[4] Their technique has the advantage of looking toward the point of decision and providing an estimate of how decision makers will respond to an issue. Essentially, the analyst would assign scores to each decision participant, weighting him or her in terms of four factors: salience of the issue, power within the group, issue position, and expected interaction with the other participants. Obviously, under this approach, the quantitative results must be treated carefully and tentatively. To invoke this procedure at each decision point in the policy process would be exceptionally cumbersome and ultimately misleading. Nonetheless, the perspective promoted by the technique at least points the analyst in the right direction.

In an article that touches on the major problem addressed by this book, Peter J. May has noted the difficulty of integrating what he terms "pure" policy analysis with politics.[5] Despite the increase in analytical capacities, a salient feasibility gap remains between the proposals of analysts and their political acceptance and administrative implementation. May suggests that the analyst think in terms of "perceptual maps" and "position maps" that chart the passage of an issue through the policy process.[6] These techniques can assist the analyst to anticipate the ways in which his or her recommendations will be seen by different policy actors and the political concerns that may be aroused by them. With attention to these possibilities beforehand, analysts may be able to avoid the use of unnecessarily antagonistic language and package proposals as attractively or as innocuously as possible.

One tactic that has been effective in moving proposals through the policy process while retaining analytical integrity has been partisan analysis. Charles Lindblom describes this approach as a method for achieving agreement even though value positions differ.[7] The analyst must locate those values of the policy maker that will also be served by the recommendations that have been made. Thus, a proposal to lower taxes might be presented to business as a means of encouraging private enterprise and to unions as a means of increasing employment opportunities. The integrity of the analysis and proposal remains unsullied, but policy actors from different ideological viewpoints still find the policy worthy of support. Again, this approach requires the analyst to have the ability to project realistically beyond his or her study to the forums in which it will be considered. Partisan analysis will, of course, not be possible under all circumstances, but it does open important possibilities for the more effective use of analysis.

For the most part, the foregoing suggestions deal with questions of technique. They do not reach fundamental normative issues. They provide no guidelines for the analyst facing difficult questions in examining a problem and striving to take rationally and ethically justifiable positions.

Moving toward the Public Good

In American culture, two concepts of individualism seem to work at cross-purposes in a wide spectrum of policy questions. Here they have been called a "politics of interest" and a "politics of conscience." Abstract in their thrust, both streams of thought and attitude militate against the adequate conceptualization and treatment of problems of policy. Utilitarian policies, oriented to economic growth, sometimes threaten to destroy ecological integrity. At the same time, an exaggerated concern for individuals embodied in welfare spending may obscure necessities of the common good. As Charles Anderson has asked hypothetically, "Would one uphold the ideal of a free market choice in the face of irreversible environmental destruction? Or pursue equality to the point that no one had the incentive to lift a plow again?"[8] The deep-rooted habits of a political culture are not readily changed. But if there are in a culture secondary ideas and attitudes that run counter to the problematic ones, something of a cure might be wrought by heightening their influence.

Fortunately, American culture has an antibody to the dilemmas posed by a politics of conscience and a politics of interest. It is pragmatism, a habit of the American mind that brings a public into being, and organizes its energies for political action. As John Dewey has written:

The characteristic of the public as a state springs from the fact that all modes of associated behavior may have extensive and enduring consequences which involve others beyond those directly engaged in them. When these consequences are in turn realized in thought and sentiment, recognition of them reacts to remake the conditions out of which they arose. Consequences have to be taken care of, looked out for.[9]

Thus, while an individual eagerness to make money creates Love Canals, the alerted public legislates into existence an Environmental Protection Agency to clean them up. The case-by-case method of the American common-law tradition reinforces this atheoretical attitude.

The responses of the pragmatic spirit operate without benefit of an overarching theory of the good. They meet the public need in terms of the specific elements of a particular situation. Pragmatism is particularist and situation oriented in its ethic.[10] Unlike utilitarianism and deontology, it does not start with an ideal theory and attempt to derive proposals for policy from it. As Charles Anderson has put it, the pragmatist approach is to "begin from practice and apply theory to it. Philosophic pragmatists have frequently suggested that principles 'emerge' out of the consideration of a particular problem of judgment."[11] The cultivation of pragmatism may help move policy makers toward a flexibility in policy assessment that will overcome the rigidities created by the other, less flexible attitudes that tend to dominate the American mind. It may help to establish an ongoing discourse among these other ideas, a conversation among utilitarians and deontologists that will allow the the frameworks for policy analysis and policy decisions to be tailored to the requirements of the particular situation. This way of applying theory to practice requires a conclusion as to

whether there is a public interest in a specific form of association or collective project. Given the presumption in favor of autonomous collective action, the burden of the argument falls to those who would give good reasons for the suppression or control of practices, or alternatively, their protection and promotion through state action.[12]

This is one way of freeing students of public policy from the value prejudices implicit in the systematic frameworks that have come with the business of policy analysis. Standing back from habitual predispositions, whether the utilitarianism of cost-benefit analysis or the egalitarian Kantianism of welfarism, forces one to look at the policy situation in its multifaceted complexity and pragmatically decide what must be done for the public good.

Not all of the suggestions in these concluding remarks are within the control of the analyst, but some of them are. In this latter regard, the analyst can greatly improve the effect of his or her efforts by basing them on a thorough understanding of the policy process and the cultural contradictions on which it rests. If policy analysts can combine this perspective with a pragmatic approach to specific issues, they should reasonably expect that in most circumstances they will be able to enhance the utilization of rational analysis in policy decisions.

Notes

1. Robert E. DiClerico and Eric Uslaner, *Few Are Chosen: Problems in Presidential Selection* (New York: McGraw-Hill, 1984), 194.

2. James MacGregor Burns, *The Power to Lead: The Crisis of the American Presidency* (New York: Simon and Schuster, 1984), 198.

3. Ibid., 199.

4. William D. Coplin and Michael K. O'Leary, *Everyman's Prince: A Guide to Understanding Your Political Problems*, rev. ed. (North Scituate, Mass.: Duxbury Press, 1976).

5. Peter J. May, "Politics and Policy Analysis," *Political Science Quarterly* 101 (Spring 1986): 114.

6. Ibid., 122–25.

7. Charles E. Lindblom, *The Policy-Making Process*, 2nd ed. (Englewood Cliffs, N.J.: Prentice-Hall, 1980), 28–32, 48.

8. Charles Anderson, "Political Philosophy, Practical Reason, and Policy Analysis" (paper presented at American Political Science Association meeting, Washington, D.C., 1984), 10.

9. John Dewey, *The Public and Its Problems* (Chicago: Swallow Press, 1946), 27.

10. The approach suggested here is also similar to that of Julius Kovesi. See Julius Kovesi, *Moral Notions* (New York: Humanities Press, 1967).

11. Anderson, "Political Philosophy," 15.

12. Ibid.

Index

About the Authors

Robert A. Heineman is Professor of Political Science at Alfred University, where he has taught for eighteen years. He received his Ph.D. from The American University. He has served on national, state, and local levels of government. His major publications include *Authority and the Liberal Tradition* (1984) and numerous articles in social science journals.

William T. Bluhm is Professor of Political Science at the University of Rochester, where he has taught for thirty-two years. He received his Ph.D. from the University of Chicago. His major publications include *Theories of the Political System* (1965, 1972, 1978), *Building an Austrian Nation* (1973), *Ideologies and Attitudes* (1974), and *Force or Freedom?* (1984).

Steven A. Peterson is Professor of Political Science at Alfred University, where he has taught for sixteen years. He received his Ph.D. from the State University of New York at Buffalo. He is past president of the New York State Political Science Association. His major publications include articles in the *Journal of Politics*, the *American Journal of Political Science*, and the *Western Political Quarterly*.

Edward N. Kearny is Professor of Government at Western Kentucky University, where he has taught for twenty years. He received his Ph.D. from The American University. His major publications include *Thurman Arnold* (1970), *Mavericks in American Politics* (1976), and an edited volume, *Dimensions of the Modern Presidency* (1981).